CH00793040

Microsoft® Office Visio® Professional 2007

Level 2

Microsoft® Office Visio® Professional 2007: Level 2

Part Number: 084902
Course Edition: 1.1

NOTICES

DISCLAIMER: While Element K Corporation takes care to ensure the accuracy and quality of these materials, we cannot guarantee their accuracy, and all materials are provided without any warranty whatsoever, including, but not limited to, the implied warranties of merchantability or fitness for a particular purpose. The name used in the data files for this course is that of a fictitious company. Any resemblance to current or future companies is purely coincidental. We do not believe we have used anyone's name in creating this course, but if we have, please notify us and we will change the name in the next revision of the course. Element K is an independent provider of integrated training solutions for individuals, businesses, educational institutions, and government agencies. Use of screenshots, photographs of another entity's products, or another entity's product name or service in this book is for editorial purposes only. No such use should be construed to imply sponsorship or endorsement of the book by, nor any affiliation of such entity with Element K. This courseware may contain links to sites on the Internet that are owned and operated by third parties (the "External Sites"). Element K is not responsible for the availability of, or the content located on or through, any External Site. Please contact Element K if you have any concerns regarding such links or External Sites.

TRADEMARK NOTICES Element K and the Element K logo are trademarks of Element K Corporation and its affiliates.

Microsoft® Office Visio® Professional 2007 is a registered trademark of Microsoft Corporation in the U.S. and other countries; the Microsoft products and services discussed or described may be trademarks of Microsoft Corporation. All other product names and services used throughout this course may be common law or registered trademarks of their respective proprietors.

Copyright © 2009 Element K Corporation. All rights reserved. Screenshots used for illustrative purposes are the property of the software proprietor. This publication, or any part thereof, may not be reproduced or transmitted in any form or by any means, electronic or mechanical, including photocopying, recording, storage in an information retrieval system, or otherwise, without express written permission of Element K, 500 Canal View Boulevard, Rochester, NY 14623, (585) 240-7500, (800) 478-7788. Element K Courseware's World Wide Web site is located at **www.elementkcourseware.com**.

This book conveys no rights in the software or other products about which it was written; all use or licensing of such software or other products is the responsibility of the user according to terms and conditions of the owner. Do not make illegal copies of books or software. If you believe that this book, related materials, or any other Element K materials are being reproduced or transmitted without permission, please call (800) 478-7788.

Your comments are important to us. Please contact us at Element K Press LLC, 1-800-478-7788, 500 Canal View Boulevard, Rochester, NY 14623, Attention: Product Planning, or through our Web site at **http://support.elementkcourseware.com**.

Microsoft® Office Visio® Professional 2007: Level 2

About This Course

Microsoft® Office Visio® Professional 2007: Level 2 is the second course in the Microsoft Visio 2007 series. In Microsoft® Office Visio® Professional 2007: Level 1, you used the various templates to design and manage workflows and flowcharts. This course will build upon the knowledge gained, and enable you to work with many advanced features, including using the drawing tools, creating and working with custom stencils and templates, and sharing your Visio drawings with other applications.

When an architect builds a house, he starts with the foundation and then adds complex structures to complete it. Learning an application is similar to this. You can start with learning the basics of the software; however, learning the advanced options would enable you to build a complete document. The Microsoft® Office Visio® Professional 2007: Level 2 course would help build on the fundamentals learned in the Microsoft® Office Visio® Professional 2007: Level 1 course.

Course Description

Target Student

This course is designed for individuals who have an understanding of the basic workflow and the concept of end-to-end flowcharting.

Course Prerequisites

Students should be familiar with personal computers, mouse, and keyboard (basic typing skills are recommended). They should be comfortable in the Windows environment and be able to use Windows to manage information on their computers. Specifically, they should be able to launch and close programs, navigate to information stored on the computer, and manage files and folders. Apart from these, the user should be familiar with Microsoft® Office Visio® Professional 2007: Level 1. Also, a basic knowledge of Microsoft Word, Excel, and Access would be helpful, but is not required.

How to Use This Book

As a Learning Guide

Each lesson covers one broad topic or set of related topics. Lessons are arranged in order of increasing proficiency with *Microsoft® Visio 2007*; skills you acquire in one lesson are used and developed in subsequent lessons. For this reason, you should work through the lessons in sequence.

Each lesson is organized into results-oriented topics. Topics include all the relevant and supporting information you need to master *Microsoft® Visio 2007*, and activities allow you to apply this information to practical hands-on examples.

You get to try out each new skill on a specially prepared sample file. This saves you typing time and allows you to concentrate on the skill at hand. Through the use of sample files, hands-on activities, illustrations that give you feedback at crucial steps, and supporting background information, this book provides you with the foundation and structure to learn *Microsoft® Visio 2007* quickly and easily.

As a Review Tool

Any method of instruction is only as effective as the time and effort you are willing to invest in it. In addition, some of the information that you learn in class may not be important to you immediately, but it may become important later on. For this reason, you are encouraged to spend some time reviewing the topics and activities after the course. For additional challenge when reviewing activities, try the "What You Do" column before looking at the "How You Do It" column.

As a Reference

The organization and layout of the book make it easy to use as a learning tool and as an after-class reference. You can use this book as a first source for definitions of terms, background information on given topics, and summaries of procedures.

Course Icons

Icon	Description
	A **Caution Note** makes students aware of potential negative consequences of an action, setting, or decision that are not easily known.
	Display Slide provides a prompt to the instructor to display a specific slide. Display Slides are included in the Instructor Guide only.
	An **Instructor Note** is a comment to the instructor regarding delivery, classroom strategy, classroom tools, exceptions, and other special considerations. Instructor Notes are included in the Instructor Guide only.
	Notes Page indicates a page that has been left intentionally blank for students to write on.
	A **Student Note** provides additional information, guidance, or hints about a topic or task.
	A **Version Note** indicates information necessary for a specific version of software.

Course Objectives

In this course, you will create custom elements and a custom template, represent external data as a drawing, and share your work with others.

You will:

● create a custom shape.
● design a custom stencil.
● design styles and templates.
● design a floor plan.
● represent external data in Visio.
● share your drawings.

Course Requirements

Hardware

To use Microsoft® Office Visio® Professional 2007 on a student's machine, you need the following:

- Intel® Pentium® 1.64 GHz or a higher processor
- 512 megabytes (MB) of RAM or more
- 15 gigabytes (GB) of available hard-disk space or more
- CD-ROM drive or DVD ROM
- Super VGA or higher resolution monitor
- Microsoft Mouse, Microsoft IntelliMouse®, or a compatible pointing device
- A printer
- A projection system to display the instructor's computer screen
- Additional items or services are required to use certain features: such as 14.4 Kbps or a faster modem, and a multimedia computer to access sound and other multimedia effects

Software

Software required on each machine includes the following:

- Microsoft® Windows Vista™ Business Edition or Microsoft Windows XP Professional
- Microsoft® Office Visio® Professional 2007
- Microsoft® Office Professional Edition 2007

Class Setup

Install Windows Vista Business Edition

To install Windows Vista Business Edition:

1. Boot your computer with the DVD containing Business Edition.
2. In the **Install Windows** window, click **Next** to continue the setup.

 This course has been developed with the **Time and Currency** format set as **English (United States)**.

3. Click the **Install Now** button.
4. In the **Product Key** text box, type the product key of your software and click **Next** to continue.
5. Accept the license agreement and click **Next** to continue.
6. On the **Which Type Of Installation Do You Want** screen, select **Custom (Advanced)**.
7. In the **Where do you Want to Install Windows** window, create new partitions with a minimum capacity of 15 GB. Format the partitions to NTFS.
8. Select the C drive partition to install Windows Vista and click **Next** to continue.

9. The computer will automatically restart after a few minutes. Remove the DVD before the system restarts.

10. After finalizing the setup, the computer will restart once again.

11. In the **Type A User Name** text box, enter an account name of *User##*, where ## is a unique number between 1 and 10. Name the Instructor's user account *User100.*

12. In the **Type A Password** text box, type *p@ssw0rd.*

13. In the **Retype A Password** text box, retype the password to confirm the login details.

14. In the **Type A Password Hint** text box, type *p@ssw0rd* and click **Next** to continue.

15. In the **Type A Computer Name** text box, type a name for the computer. For the instructor's computer, name the computer *Computer100.* For the student's computer, name each one *COMPUTER##*, where ## is a unique number between 1 and 10–adjust the range accordingly for the number of students in the class.

16. Click **Next** to continue.

17. On the **Help Protect Windows Automatically** screen, click **Use Recommended Settings.**

18. Specify your time and date settings.

   ■ From the **Time Zone** drop-down list, select your time zone.

   ■ In the **Date** section, set the current date.

   ■ If necessary, modify the system time.

19. Click **Next** to continue.

20. On the **Select Your Computer's Current Location** screen, click **Work.**

21. On the **Thank You** screen, click **Start** to start working with Windows Vista.

22. In the **Password** text box, type *p@ssw0rd* and press **Enter.**

Activate Windows Vista

To activate Windows Vista:

1. Choose **start→Control Panel→System And Maintenance.**

2. Click **System.**

3. In the **Windows Activation** section, click **Activate Windows Now.**

4. If prompted, click **Continue.**

5. In the **Windows Activation** dialog box, click **Activate Windows Online Now.**

6. On the **Activation was Successful** page, click **Close.**

Provide Administrator Rights

To provide administrator rights:

1. On the **start** menu, right-click **Computer** and choose **Manage.**

2. In the **User Account Control** dialog box, click **Continue.**

3. In the **Computer Management (Local)** pane, choose **Local Users and Groups→Users.**

4. In the center pane, right-click **Administrator** and choose **Properties.**

5. In the **Administrator Properties** dialog box, uncheck the **Account is disabled** check box and click **OK.**

6. Choose **start→Computer.**

7. Right-click **Local Disk (C:)** and choose **Properties.**

8. In the **Local Disk (C:) Properties** dialog box, on the **Security** tab, click **Edit.**

9. Click **Add.**

10. In the **Select Users or Groups** dialog box, click **Advanced** and then click **Find Now.**

11. In the **Search results** section, select **Everyone** and click **OK** two times.

12. In the **Permission for Local Disk (C:)** dialog box, in the **Permission for Everyone** section, in the **Allow** column, check the **Full Control** check box.

13. Click **Apply** and then click **OK** two times.

Install Microsoft Office Professional Plus 2007

To install Microsoft Office Professional Plus 2007:

1. Double-click the **setup.exe** file.

2. Enter the product key and click **Continue.**

3. Accept the license agreement and click **Continue.**

4. Click **Install Now.**

5. Once the installation is complete, click **Close.**

Install Microsoft Office Visio Professional 2007

To install Microsoft Office Visio Professional 2007:

1. Double-click the **setup.exe** file.

2. Enter the product key and click **Continue.**

3. Accept the license agreement and click **Continue.**

4. Click **Install Now.**

5. Once the installation is complete, click **Close.**

Initial Class Setup

1. On the course CD-ROM, run the **084902dd.exe** self-extracting file. This will install a folder named **084902Data** on your C drive. This folder contains all the data files that you will use to complete this course.

2. Provide each student with Administrator rights.

If your book did not come with a CD, please go to **http:// www.elementk.com/ courseware-file-downloads** to download the data files.

3. Verify that file extensions are visible. In Windows Explorer, choose **Organize→Folder and Search Options** and select the **View** tab. If necessary, uncheck the **Hide Extensions For Known File Types** check box and click **OK.**

4. If necessary, Choose **start→Control Panel→User Accounts,** and click the **Go to main User Accounts page** link. On the **Make changes to your user account** page, click the **Turn User Account Control on or off** link and uncheck the **Use User Account Control (UAC) to help protect your computer** check box. Click **OK** to provide all users complete administrative rights.

5. Install a printer of your choice.

List of Additional Files

Printed with each activity is a list of files students open to complete that activity. Many activities also require additional files that students do not open, but are needed to support the file(s) students are working with. These supporting files are included with the student data files on the course CD-ROM or data disk. Do not delete these files.

1

Creating a Custom Shape

Lesson Time: 45 minutes

Lesson Objectives:

In this lesson, you will create a custom shape.

You will:

- Draw basic shapes.
- Enhance basic shapes.

Introduction

You have worked with various master shapes using different stencils. However, these stencil masters may not always cater to your specific needs. In this lesson, you will create a custom shape.

Shapes are the most basic and integral part of Visio. Regardless of the type of drawing you are working on, you can use the different shapes provided. However, while working on the design of an application, you may be unable to customize the predefined shapes to match your needs. Rather than trying to work on the given shapes, you can create a shape of your own to suit your personal needs.

TOPIC A
Draw Basic Shapes

You are equipped with the skill of creating a basic workflow drawing. Sometimes, you may need to enhance your drawing with unique basic shapes. In this topic, you will draw a basic shape.

Children use a variety of building blocks in their play. Each small block helps them create a new model. Likewise, learning to draw basic shapes will strengthen your abilities to create complex custom shapes.

Types of Shapes

Shapes can be broadly classified as open and closed shapes. An *open shape* is a shape that is created from a line or an arc, but contains endpoints that are not connected. You can apply line formatting to an open shape, but you cannot apply a fill or a pattern. A *free form shape* is also a type of open shape. A *closed shape* is one that is surrounded by a continuous outline, such as a rectangle or a circle. Closed shapes can be filled with a color or a pattern.

A free form shape is one whose exact figure cannot be described. Shapes that are drawn freely using the mouse are examples of free form shape.

Drawing Tools

The drawing tools enable us to draw both open and closed shapes. These tools are located on the **Drawing** toolbar.

Drawing Tool	Purpose
Rectangle tool	Enables users to create square and rectangular shapes.
Ellipse tool	Enables users to create oval and circular shapes.
Line tool	Enables users to create basic lines. It can also be used to create lines with multiple segments. Holding **Shift** while using this tool restricts the tool to draw lines at an angle of 45°.
Arc tool	Enables users to create arched and curved lines. It can also be used to create curves with multiple segments.
Freeform tool	Enables users to create multi-segment curved lines. It is used to create curves by drawing freely with the mouse.

Drawing Tool	*Purpose*
Pencil tool	Enables users to draw both straight and curved lines. It can also be used to reshape existing lines and shapes.

 Holding **Shift** while using the **Rectangle** or **Ellipse** tool enables you to draw proportional shapes.

How to Draw Basic Shapes

Procedure Reference: Add a Toolbar to the Interface

To add a toolbar to the interface:

1. Open a drawing in the Visio application.
2. Display the **Customize** dialog box.
   - Choose **Tools→Customize.**
   - Choose **View→Toolbars→Customize.**
   - Or, right-click any toolbar and choose **Customize.**
3. In the **Customize** dialog box, on the **Toolbars** tab, in the **Toolbars** list box, check the toolbar you want to display.
4. Click **Close** to add the toolbar to the interface.

 Another method to add a toolbar to the interface is, right-clicking the toolbar section and choosing the desired toolbar from the shortcut menu.

Procedure Reference: Draw Basic Shapes

To draw basic shapes:

1. Add the **Drawing** toolbar to the interface.
2. On the **Drawing** toolbar, click the desired drawing tool.
3. Drag to draw a shape on the drawing page.
4. If necessary, modify the attributes of the shape using the **Size & Position** window.

ACTIVITY 1-1

Drawing Basic Shapes

Data Files:

OGC Basic.vsd

Before You Begin:

From the C:\084902Data\Creating A Custom Shape folder, open the OGC Basic.vsd file.

Scenario:

While working on your flowchart, you decide to add your organization's logo to it. Since the first shape you create determines the final product, you start by adding a few basic shapes.

What You Do	How You Do It
1. Display the **Drawing** toolbar.	a. Choose **Tools→Customize.**
	b. In the **Customize** dialog box, on the **Toolbars** tab, in the **Toolbars** list box, check the **Drawing** check box, and click **Close.**
	c. If necessary, dock the **Drawing** toolbar near the **Standard** toolbar.
2. Draw a square of 2-inch dimension.	a. On the **Drawing** toolbar, click the **Rectangle** tool.
	b. Place the cross hair mouse pointer at **X=1** inches and **Y=10** inches, hold down **Shift** and drag to draw a square of 2-inch dimension.
3. Make nine copies of the square.	a. Verify that the square is selected.
	b. Hold down **Ctrl** and drag the instance of the square 1 inch to the right of the square.

c. Similarly, make eight more instances of the square and arrange them in sequence on the drawing page.

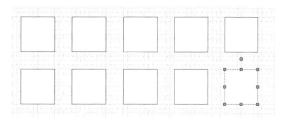

4. Modify the **Angle** attribute of the squares.

a. Display the **Size & Position** window.

b. Select the first square.

c. In the **Size & Position** window, change the **Angle** attribute to *10* and press **Enter.**

d. Select the second square and change its **Angle** attribute to *20* and press **Enter.**

e. Similarly, change the **Angle** attribute of the remaining eight squares with a difference of 10 degree each.

f. Select the **Pointer** tool.

g. Position the second square on top of the first square.

h. Similarly, position the remaining eight squares one on top of the other.

i. Save the file as *My OGC Basic.vsd* in the **C:\084902Data\Creating A Custom Shape** folder and close it.

TOPIC B
Enhance Basic Shapes

You have created basic shapes. Formatting these shapes adds to the visual appeal. In this topic, you will enhance the basic shapes, thus creating a custom shape.

While representing content as shapes or images, you may not always find the shape you need among the built-in shapes provided by the application. Formatting these shapes can be extremely time consuming. Rather than wasting your time trying to customize the predefined shapes, you can manipulate basic shapes to create one of your own.

The Shape Operation Commands

The shape operation commands enable you to create a new shape from two or more overlapping shapes. These commands can be accessed from the **Operations** submenu of the **Shape** menu.

Option	*Used To*
Union	Create a shape from overlapping shapes using the perimeter of all the shapes involved as the outline.
Combine	Create a shape from overlapping shapes by removing the areas that overlap.
Fragment	Create numerous shapes by breaking the overlapping shapes along the lines where they overlap.
Intersect	Create a shape from only the area that overlaps and deletes the remaining area.
Subtract	Create a shape by removing the area that overlaps the selected shape.

Other Shape Operation Commands

Apart from the above mentioned shape operation commands, a few shape operation commands enable you to create a new shape by modifying the existing single shape. The following table lists the other shape operation commands.

Command	*Description*
Join	Creates a shape by aligning individual segments into one or more continuous paths.
Trim	Splits selected shapes at their intersection, thereby creating a new shape.
Offset	Creates a set of parallel lines or curves to the right or left of the original shape.
Fit Curve	Curves the vertices of a closed shape.

How to Enhance Basic Shapes

Procedure Reference: Add Commands to the Toolbar

To add commands to the toolbar:

1. If necessary, open a drawing.

2. Display the **Customize** dialog box.

3. In the **Customize** dialog box, on the **Commands** tab, in the **Categories** list box, select the desired category to display the corresponding commands.

4. In the **Commands** list box, select the desired command and drag to the toolbar to add the command to the toolbar.

5. If necessary, right-click the commands and choose **Begin a Group** to organize the commands into a new group.

6. Click **Close** to close the **Customize** dialog box.

Procedure Reference: Modify a Basic Shape

To modify a basic shape:

1. Open the desired drawing.

2. If necessary, add shapes to the drawing page.

3. Align the shapes.

    a. Choose **Shape→Align** to display the **Align Shapes** dialog box.

    b. In the **Align Shapes** dialog box, select the desired vertical and horizontal alignment.

    c. If necessary, check the **Create guide and glue shapes to it** check box to align shapes easily at a later point.

    d. Click **OK.**

4. Choose **Shape→Operations** and then choose the desired shape operation commands to modify the shape. The commands include **Union, Combine, Fragment, Intersect,** and **Subtract.**

5. If necessary, format the custom shape.

ACTIVITY 1-2

Enhancing Basic Shapes

Data Files:

OGC Logo.vsd

Before You Begin:

From the C:\084902Data\Creating A Custom Shape folder, open the OGC Logo.vsd file.

Scenario:

You took a break after drawing your basic shapes. Now, you wish to continue working on them, formatting and enhancing the shapes, to create your logo.

What You Do	How You Do It
1. Add the shape operation commands to the **Action** toolbar.	a. Display the **Customize** dialog box.
	b. On the **Toolbars** tab, check the **Action** check box.
	c. Select the **Commands** tab.
	d. In the **Categories** list box, select **Shape Operations** to display the corresponding commands in the **Commands** list box.
	e. In the **Commands** list box, scroll down and drag the **Union** command to the right corner of the **Action** toolbar.

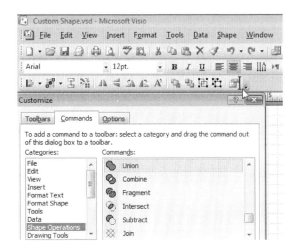

f. Similarly, add the **Combine, Fragment, Intersect,** and **Subtract** commands to the right of the **Union** command.

g. Click **Close.**

2. Combine the ten squares to form a single shape.

    a. Select all the shapes.

    b. On the **Action** toolbar, click the **Combine** button.

3. Create a new shape on **Page-2.**

    a. Display **Page-2.**

    b. Select the **Rectangle** tool.

    c. Position the cross hair mouse pointer at **X=2** inches and **Y=7** inches and then draw a square of 2-inch dimension.

    d. Using the **Size & Position** window, change the **Angle** of the square to *45* and press **Enter.**

    e. Position the cross hair mouse pointer at **X=5** inches and **Y=7** inches and then draw a circle of 1.5-inch dimension.

    f. Copy the circle and place it to the right of the current circle.

    g. Using the **Size & Position** window, change the width and height of the second circle to *1 in*

    h. Select all the shapes.

    i. Choose **Shape→Align Shapes.**

    j. In the **Align Shapes** dialog box, in both the **Vertical alignment** and **Horizontal alignment** sections, select the center alignment options and click **OK.**

4. Format the fragmented shape.

a. Click the blank area on the drawing page to deselect the shapes.

b. On the **Drawing** toolbar, click the **Pencil** tool.

c. Position the pencil mouse pointer half an inch above the top vertex of the square and draw a line through the shapes such that it intersects the shapes and is half an inch outside the shape.

d. Click the blank area on the drawing page to deselect the shapes.

e. Select all the shapes.

f. On the **Action** toolbar, click the **Fragment** button.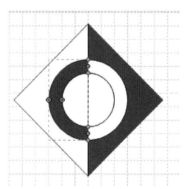

g. If necessary, click the right side of the square to select it.

h. On the **Formatting** toolbar, from the **Fill Color** drop-down list, in the **Standard Colors** section, select the **Dark Blue** color.

i. Select the outer circle on the left and fill it with the same color.

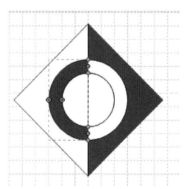

j. Select the square on the left and from the **Fill Color** drop-down list, from the **Theme Colors** section, in the second column on the right, select **Light Blue Shade 10%.**

k. Select the outer circle on the right and color it with **Light Blue Shade 10%.**

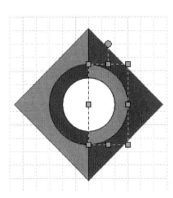

5. Combine the shapes to form a custom shape.

a. Select all the shapes.

b. On the **Action** toolbar, click the **Group** button.

c. Right-click the shape and choose **Copy.**

d. Display **Page-1.**

e. Right-click the drawing page and choose **Paste.**

f. Select the **Pointer** tool and position the copied shape inside the circle.

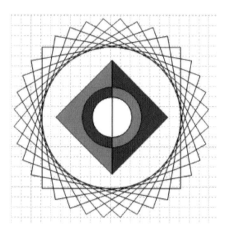

g. Position the cross hair mouse pointer at **X=0.5** inches and **Y=8.25** inches and then draw a square of 5.25-inch dimension over the custom shape.

h. Right-click the square and choose **Shape→Send to Back.**

i. If necessary, position the other shapes in the center of the square.

6. Format the logo.

    a. Verify that the outer square is selected.

    b. On the **Formatting** toolbar, from the **Fill Color** drop-down list, in the second column on the right, select **Light Blue Tint 35%.**

    c. Select the innermost circle and fill it with **Light Blue Tint 35%.**

    d. Select the outer square.

    e. Change the **Angle** of the shape to *45* and press **Enter.**

    f. Select all the shapes.

    g. On the **Action** toolbar, click the **Group** button.

    h. Using the **Size & Position** window, resize the shape to *2 in* dimension.

    i. Save the file as *My OGC Logo.vsd* and close it.

Lesson 1 Follow-up

In this lesson, you created a custom shape. By creating a custom shape, you saved the time and effort required to customize a stencil master.

1. **On your job, what kind of custom shapes would you require to create?**

2. **Of the drawing tools available, which tool do you think is most beneficial in creating a custom shape?**

2 | Designing a Custom Stencil

Lesson Time: 35 minutes

Lesson Objectives:

In this lesson, you will design a custom stencil.

You will:

- Create a custom stencil.
- Customize a stencil master.

Introduction

You have created custom shapes. Now, you may want to use these shapes in other drawings rather than create them each time. In this lesson, you will design a custom stencil that contains the custom master.

Although Visio has several components to match your needs in a drawing, there might be several instances wherein you would have created complex shapes. Also, there may be a need to use these complex shapes in many of your drawings. So, preserving these complex shapes, rather than re-creating them, would save you time.

TOPIC A
Create a Custom Stencil

You have added numerous shapes while creating drawings in Visio. However, there maybe certain shapes that you constantly use across all drawings. In this topic, you will create a custom stencil that holds the shapes you often use.

Visio provides a variety of shapes that, when placed on the drawing page, help represent different components. However, sometimes the component that you need may not be available, forcing you to draw your own shape. There may also be instances wherein you want to use a particular shape repeatedly. Being able to reuse the shapes that you created helps save time.

Document Stencils

A *Document Stencil* is a stencil that contains the masters of all shapes used in that particular drawing. Each Visio drawing will have a distinct document stencil based on the different shapes used in that drawing. When a shape is dragged onto the drawing page, Visio creates a copy of the master in the **Document Stencil**. Also, editing a master in the **Document Stencil** ensures that all instances of the shape are modified accordingly. Thus, the shapes inherit the formatting and other properties from the master on the **Document Stencil**.

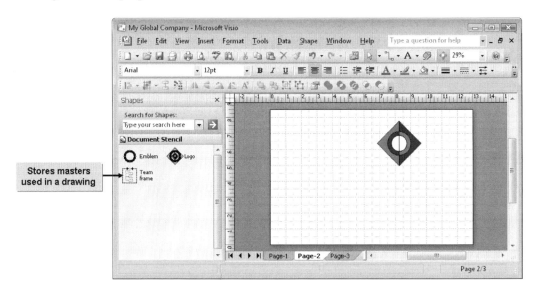

Figure 2-1: The Shapes window displaying the Document Stencil.

How to Create a Custom Stencil

Procedure Reference: Create a Custom Stencil

To create a custom stencil:

1. Choose **File→Shapes→New Stencil (US Units)** to create a new stencil.

2. Right-click the title bar of the newly created stencil and choose **Save.**

3. In the **Save As** dialog box, in the **File name** text box, type the desired name.

4. If necessary, navigate to the desired location.

5. Click **Save** to save the custom stencil.

 You can lock or unlock stencils anytime by clicking the stencil icon on the title bar and choosing **Edit Stencil.** Stencils must be unlocked in order to add new masters or edit existing masters in the window.

6. If necessary, right-click the title bar of the customized stencil and choose **Edit Stencil** to lock the stencil.

Procedure Reference: Copy Shapes to the Custom Stencil

To copy shapes to the custom stencil:

1. Choose **File→Shapes→New Stencil** and choose the custom stencil.

2. On the drawing page, select the shape you want to copy to the custom stencil.

3. Hold down **Ctrl,** and drag the shape to the stencil.

4. Right-click the shape on the stencil and choose **Edit Master→Master Properties.**

5. In the **Master Properties** dialog box, in the **Properties** section, in the **Name** text box, type the desired name for the shape.

6. Click **OK.**

7. Right-click the title bar of the custom stencil and choose **Save** to save the changes.

8. If necessary, copy a shape from the **Document Stencil** of another file.

   a. Choose **Window→Tile** to display both the windows together.

   b. Choose **File→Shapes→Show Document Stencil** to display the **Document Stencil.**

   c. From the **Document Stencil,** drag the desired shape to the custom stencil. The shape gets copied to the custom stencil.

   d. Save the changes to the custom stencil.

Undock Stencils

While working on a drawing, you may sometimes find it more comfortable to have the stencil that you want located in some other location rather than the left corner. To undock the desired stencil, you can right-click the title bar of the stencil and choose **Float Window.** This stencil can now be moved around anywhere on the drawing page, or can be docked in another location to suit your needs.

ACTIVITY 2-1

Creating a Custom Stencil

Data Files:

Global Company.vsd, Org Chart.vsd

Before You Begin:

From the C:\084902Data\Designing A Custom Stencil folder, open the Global Company.vsd file.

Scenario:

Your organization is a part of the corporate cultural festival. You are the leader for your team—The Red Rangers. You have decided to use your organization's logo as your emblem for the festival. You also wish to save the changes you make so that you can use it in all future drawings. To enhance your logo, you further plan to camouflage it with the logo you had used the previous year.

What You Do	How You Do It
1. Create a custom stencil.	a. Choose **File→Shapes→New Stencil (US Units).**
	b. Observe that a new stencil titled **Stencil1** is added in the **Shapes** window and the stencil icon in the left corner of the title bar shows a small red asterisk.
	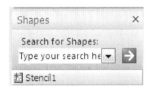
	c. Right-click the title bar of **Stencil1** and choose **Save** to display the **Save As** dialog box.
	d. In the **Save As** dialog box, in the **File name** text box, type *Our Global Company*
	e. Verify that the location of saving the custom stencil is **Student\Documents\My Shapes.**
	While working on a Windows XP system, the stencil will be saved in the **C:\Users\Student\My Documents\My Shapes** folder.
	f. Click **Save** to save the custom stencil.
2. Lock the stencil.	a. Right-click the title bar of the **Our Global Company** stencil and choose **Edit Stencil.**
	b. Observe that the red asterisk is not visible any more.
	c. Right-click the title bar of the **Our Global Company** stencil and choose **Close** to close the stencil.

3. Copy a shape to the custom stencil.

a. Choose **File→Shapes→My Shapes→Our Global Company.**

b. Right-click the title bar of the **Our Global Company** stencil and choose **Edit Stencil** to unlock the stencil.

c. Click any corner of the square to select the shape.

d. Copy the shape and place it on the **Our Global Company** stencil.

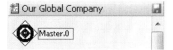

e. Verify that the shape is selected and on the **Action** toolbar, click the **Ungroup** button.

f. Click over the circumference that forms the outer largest circle to select that shape.

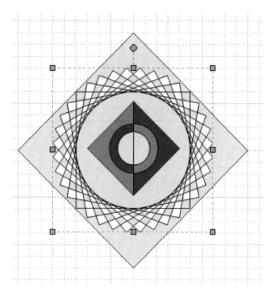

g. Copy the shape and place it on the **Our Global Company** stencil.

h. Select the outer largest circle on the drawing page and press **Delete.**

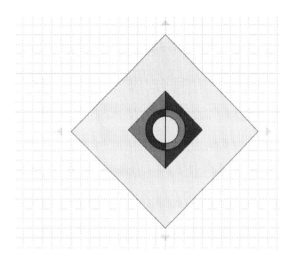

i. Select all the shapes and on the **Action** toolbar, click the **Group** button.

j. On the drawing page, verify that the shape is selected and copy it to the **Our Global Company** stencil.

---

4. Name the master shapes.

a. On the **Our Global Company** stencil, right-click the **Master.0** shape and choose **Edit Master→Master Properties** to display the **Master Properties** dialog box.

b. In the **Properties** section, in the **Name** text box, type *Logo* and click **OK.**

c. Display the **Master Properties** dialog box, and name **Master.1** as *Emblem*

d. Similarly, name **Master.2** as *Badge*

e. On the title bar of the **Our Global Company** stencil, click the **Save Stencil** button.

---

5. Add shapes from the **Document Stencil** to **Our Global Company.**

a. From the **C:\084902Data\Designing A Custom Stencil** folder, open the Org Chart.vsd file.

b. Choose **Window→Tile** to display all the windows together.

c. Choose **File→Shapes→Show Document Stencil** to display the **Document Stencil.**

d. Right-click the title bar of the **Document Stencil** and choose **Float Window.**

e. Drag the **Document Stencil** to the drawing page of the **Org Chart.vsd:1** window.

f. From the **Document Stencil,** copy the **Team frame** shape to the **Our Global Company** stencil.

g. Save the changes made to the **Our Global Company** stencil.

h. Close both the Org Chart.vsd files and save the file as *My Global Company.vsd*

TOPIC B
Customize a Stencil Master

You added custom shapes as masters in your custom stencil. The master shape that you added to your custom stencil may not have the properties required for a stencil master. In this topic, you will customize a stencil master.

Although you have created custom shapes, you might still want to edit them. For example, you may wish to change the color, revise the shape, or edit the text in the shape by editing the master. By customizing a stencil master, you can add instances of the shape to a drawing and make copies of it to speed up the process in Visio.

Developer Mode

The developer mode enables users to use advanced formatting and editing options. To work in the developer mode, you will have to check the **Run in developer mode** check box on the **Advanced** tab of the **Options** dialog box.

 Running the application in the developer mode does not modify the properties of the drawing you are working on.

How to Customize a Stencil Master

Procedure Reference: Edit a Master Shape

To edit a master shape:

1. Choose **File→Shapes→My Shapes** and select the custom stencil.
2. Right-click the master shape that you want to edit and choose **Edit Master→Edit Master Shape.**
3. In the shape drawing window, edit the shape as desired.
4. Close the shape drawing window and in the **Microsoft Office Visio** message box, click **Yes** to update the master shape.

 To rename the master shape, right-click it and then choose **Rename Master.**

5. Right-click the stencil title bar and click **Save** to save the changes.
6. Right-click the master shape and choose **Edit Master→Master Properties** to display the **Master Properties** dialog box.
7. Set the desired properties.
   - In the **Properties** section, in the **Name** text box, type a name for the master shape.
   - In the **Prompt** text box, type a brief description of the master that will get displayed when the mouse pointer is placed on the shape.

8. Click **OK** to apply the changes.

9. Switch to the developer mode.

   a. Choose **Tools→Options** to display the **Options** dialog box.

   b. On the **Advanced** tab, check the **Run in developer mode** check box to switch to the developer mode, and click **OK.**

10. Add new connection points.

    a. Select the shape to be edited in the drawing.

    b. On the **Standard** toolbar, from the **Connector** tool drop-down list, select **Connection Point Tool.**

    c. Hold down **Ctrl** and click the point on the selected shape to add a new connection point.

Master Properties

The **Master Properties** dialog box sets the properties of the selected master. You can align the master's name using the **Align master name** options and can also search for shapes using the **Keywords.**

Procedure Reference: Format a Master in a Stencil

To format a master in a stencil:

1. Right-click the master shape to edit and choose **Edit Master→Edit Master Shape.**

2. If necessary, in the shape drawing window, select the shape and on the **Action** toolbar, click the **Ungroup** button to ungroup the individual shapes.

3. Deselect the shapes.

4. Click an individual shape to select it.

5. Choose **Format→Fill** to display the **Fill** dialog box.

6. In the **Fill** dialog box, make the desired changes.

7. Click **Apply** and then click **OK** to apply changes to the master shape.

Procedure Reference: Apply Behavior to a Custom Shape

To apply behavior to a custom shape:

1. Choose **Edit→Select All.**

2. If necessary, on the **Action** toolbar, click the **Group** button to group individual shapes in a master.

3. Choose **Format→Behavior** to display the **Behavior** dialog box.

4. In the **Behavior** dialog box, set the necessary standards.

   ● On the **Behavior** tab, set the desired interaction style and group behavior.

   ● On the **Double-Click** tab, set the response of the shape to a double-click action.

   ● On the **Placement** tab, set the desired placement behavior options.

 The **Group only** option in the **Behavior** dialog box is used to select the entire group of shapes; individual shapes within the group cannot be selected.

5. Click **OK** to apply behavior.

ACTIVITY 2-2

Customizing a Stencil Master

Data Files:

My Global Company.vsd

Before You Begin:

The My Global Company.vsd file is kept open.

Scenario:

You have made your organization's logo into a custom master shape. However, you want to make changes to the color of the master so that it suits your team—The Red Rangers. Apart from this, you also wish to add few other behaviors to your shape.

What You Do	How You Do It
1. Turn on the developer mode.	a. Choose **Tools→Options.**
	b. On the **Advanced** tab, in the **Advanced options** section, check the **Run in developer mode** check box.
	c. Click **OK.**
2. Edit the **Logo** master shape in the **Our Global Company** stencil.	a. Verify that the **Our Global Company** stencil is open.
	b. On the **Our Global Company** stencil, right-click the **Logo** master shape and choose **Edit Master→Edit Master Shape.**
	c. On the drawing page, select all the shapes. On the **Action** toolbar, click the **Ungroup** button.
	d. Select the outermost square.
	e. On the **Formatting** toolbar, from the **Fill Color** drop-down list, select **Red Tint 35%.**

 To select **Red Tint 35 %,** from the **Fill Color** drop-down list, select the second color in the sixth column.

Microsoft® Office Visio® Professional 2007: Level 2

f. Select the innermost circle and color it with **Red Tint 35%.**

g. Select the outermost circle and from the **Fill Color** drop-down list, in the **Standard Colors** section, select **Dark Red.**

 To select **Dark Red,** from the **Fill Color** drop-down list, select the first color in the **Standard Colors** section.

h. Select the inner square on the left and color it with **Dark Red.**

i. Similarly, color the inner circle on the right with **Dark Red.**

j. Select the inner square on the right and color it with **Red Shade 20%.**

 To select **Red Shade 20%,** from the **Fill Color** drop-down list, select the last color in the sixth column.

26 *Lesson 2: Designing a Custom Stencil*

k. Color the inner circle on the left with **Red Shade 20%.**

l. Click the blank area on the drawing page to deselect the shapes.

3. Add connection points to the master shape.

a. On the **Standard** toolbar, from the **Connector** tool drop-down list, select **Connection Point Tool.**

b. Select the shape and hold down **Ctrl** and click the top vertex of the square.

c. Hold down **Ctrl** and click the vertex on the left.

d. Similarly, add connection points to the other two vertices.

e. Close the shape drawing window.

f. In the **Microsoft Office Visio** message box, click **Yes.**

4. Combine the **Logo** and **Team frame** master shapes on a new page.

a. Choose **Insert→New Page** to display the **Page Setup** dialog box.

b. In the **Page Setup** dialog box, click **OK** to insert a new drawing page.

c. Drag and place the **Logo** master in the middle of the drawing page.

d. Using the **Size & Position** window, change the **Height** and **Width** of the shape to *3 in*

e. Drag the **Team frame** master and place it at the center of the **Logo** shape on the drawing page.

f. Double-click the text below the **Team frame** shape and type *The Red Rangers*

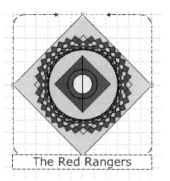

g. Using the **Formatting** toolbar, change the font size to **18 pt.**

5. Group the two master shapes.

   a. Deselect the shape.

   b. Select all the shapes.

   c. On the **Action** toolbar, click the **Group** button to group the individual shapes.

   d. Choose **Format→Behavior** to display the **Behavior** dialog box.

   e. In the **Behavior** dialog box, from the **Selection** drop-down list, select **Group only** to group the shapes together.

   f. Click **OK.**

   g. Save the changes to the **Our Global Company** stencil, and then save and close the file.

Lesson 2 Follow-up

In this lesson, you designed a custom stencil. The various techniques of creating a custom stencil will help you revise shapes and save a copy for future reference.

1. **On the job, how often would you create a custom stencil and for what purposes?**

2. **When would you turn on the developer mode option?**

3 Designing Styles and Templates

Lesson Time: 35 minutes

Lesson Objectives:

In this lesson, you will design styles and templates.

You will:

- Define a new style.
- Create a template.

Introduction

You have created a custom stencil. Using custom elements helps you easily create a drawing. In this lesson, you will design custom styles and templates.

Working in an organization might involve the use of standard logos, shapes, and colors in all your documents. Formatting each page in your document is quite cumbersome. Instead, you can create a style that can be applied uniformly to all the pages. You can also create a template that enables you to easily access the various custom tools that you created.

TOPIC A
Define a New Style

You have saved a custom stencil with a custom shape. Now, you may want all shapes in your drawings to have a similar formatting. In this topic, you will define a new style.

Your manager has requested you to give a presentation to the new employees on the organization's workflow. Since you have already created the organization's workflow, there should not be any problem preparing the presentation. As you flip through the various pages of the drawing, you notice that in each page a different style is applied to the shapes. Using Visio, you can create a style and apply it across all the pages.

Styles

In Visio, a *style* is a tool that enables you to define the appearance of a particular shape. By default, Visio provides a set of predefined styles for each shape. Using these styles, you can define the text, line, and fill of a shape. Apart from this, you can also create a custom style.

How to Define a New Style

Procedure Reference: Create a New Style

To create a new style:

1. If necessary, open a drawing.

 Ensure that no shape is selected while creating a new style. Otherwise, the style created will specifically apply to the shape selected.

2. If necessary, turn on the **Run in developer mode** option.
3. Choose **Format→Define Styles** to display the **Define Styles** dialog box.
4. In the **Styles** section, in the **Name** text box, enter the desired name for the custom style.
5. If necessary, from the **Based on** drop-down list, select a predefined style to create a new style based on existing ones.
6. Click **Add** to create the new style.
7. In the **Includes** section, uncheck the desired check box to exclude that style from the custom style.
8. In the **Change** section, set the formatting for the custom style.
    - Click the **Text** button to set the text style. In the **Text** dialog box, set the desired text formatting and click **OK.**
    - Click the **Line** button to set the line style. In the **Line** dialog box, set the desired line patterns and click **OK.**
    - Click the **Fill** button to set the fill style. In the **Fill** dialog box, set the desired fill pattern and click **OK.**
9. Click **OK** to create the custom style.

Editing a Predefined Style

Rather than create a new style from scratch, you may want to edit the properties of a preexisting style. To do this, you can use the **Style** dialog box, which can be accessed from the **Format** menu. The **Style** dialog box enables you to change the text, line, and fill of the selected style. While changing the format for the entire drawing, you can retain the manually applied formatting for the selected shape by checking the **Preserve Local Formatting** check box.

Microsoft® Office Visio® Professional 2007: Level 2

ACTIVITY 3-1

Defining a New Style

Data Files:

Conference Setup.vsd

Before You Begin:

From the C:\084902Data\Designing Styles And Templates folder, open the Conference Setup.vsd file.

Scenario:

A new employee at your organization has given you the conference hall setup that he created. On examining the drawing, you find that the shapes have different text styles and line styles applied. As your colleague wasn't aware of the organization's standard formatting, you decide to standardize the shapes to follow a particular text, line, and fill style.

What You Do	How You Do It
1. Check the text formatting of the shapes.	a. Click the text **PARKING** to check its formatting.
	b. On the **Formatting** toolbar, in the **Font** drop-down list, observe that the font for the selected text is **Algerian.**
	c. Click the text **Registration A-M.**
	d. Observe that the font for the selected text is **Arial Narrow.**
	e. Double-click **Table12.**
	f. Observe that the font for the selected text is **Britannic Bold.**

34 *Lesson 3: Designing Styles and Templates*

2. Create a new style.

    a. Click the pasteboard to deselect the selected shape.

    b. If necessary, activate the developer mode.

    c. Choose **Format→Define Styles.**

    d. In the **Define Styles** dialog box, in the **Style** section, in the **Name** text box, type *OurGlobalCompany*

    e. Click **Add.**

    f. In the **Includes** section, uncheck the **Fill** check box, so that it is not included in the style.

3. Set the text and line styles.

    a. In the **Change** section, click **Text.**

    b. In the **Text** dialog box, in the **Font settings** section, from the **Font** drop-down list, select **Times New Roman.**

    c. From the **Size** drop-down list, select **14 pt** and click **OK.**

    d. In the **Define Styles** dialog box, click **Line.**

    e. In the **Line** dialog box, in the **Line** section, from the **Weight** drop-down list, select **05:** and click **OK.**

    f. Click **OK** to close the **Define Styles** dialog box.

4. Add the **Style** drop-down list to the **Formatting** toolbar.

    a. Display the **Customize** dialog box.

    b. On the **Commands** tab, in the **Categories** list box, select **Format Shape.**

    c. In the **Commands** list box, scroll down and select the **Style** drop-down list.

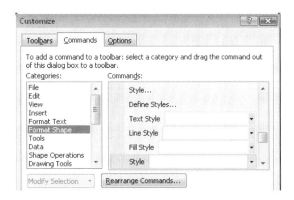

    d. Add the **Style** drop-down list to the right of the **Font Size** drop-down list on the **Formatting** toolbar.

    e. Close the **Customize** dialog box.

5. Apply the custom style to the drawing.

    a. Select all the shapes in the drawing.

    b. Hold down **Ctrl** and click the text **PARKING** to deselect the background.

    c. On the **Formatting** toolbar, from the **Style** drop-down list, select **OurGlobalCompany.**

    d. Observe that the text formatting of the drawing has changed.

    e. Save the file as *My Conference Setup.vsd* and close it.

TOPIC B

Create a Template

You have created a custom style. Like styles, the predefined templates provided in Visio sometimes may not fulfill your needs. In this topic, you will design a custom template.

Creating your own custom template gives you an easy and consistent way to incorporate custom elements into new documents. It might be your own custom logo, sections of standardized text, or a consistent set of formats. By creating a template, you can get the precise results you need for your drawings.

How to Create a Template

Procedure Reference: Create a Template

To create a template:

1. Open the drawing you want to use as the template.
2. Choose **File→Shapes** and, from the **Shapes** submenu, choose the desired stencil.
3. Choose **File→Page Setup** to modify the properties of the page.
4. If necessary, create a background page for the template.
5. If necessary, add a few shapes to the drawing page.
6. Choose **File→Save As.**
7. In the **Save As** dialog box, navigate to the desired folder location.

 To access the template file from the **Getting Started** window, click the **More** link in the **Recent Documents** pane.

8. If necessary, enter a name for the template.
9. From the **Save as type** drop-down list, select **Template (*.vst)** and click **Save** to create the custom template.

ACTIVITY 3-2

Creating a Template

Before You Begin:

Open a new drawing page.

Scenario:

Your organization has set a new policy that requires all documents to carry a watermark of your organization's name. To add a watermark to every page you create is a tedious task. Having a template with the watermark will enhance your efficiency.

What You Do	How You Do It
1. Add the custom stencil and the **Backgrounds (US units)** stencil to the drawing.	a. Choose **File→Shapes→Open Stencil.**
	b. In the **Open Stencil** dialog box, navigate to the **C:\Users\Student\Documents\My Shapes** folder.

 If you are using Windows XP, navigate to the **C:\Users\Student\My Documents\My Shapes** folder.

c. Select the **Our Global Company.vss** stencil and click **Open.**

d. Observe that the **Our Global Company** stencil has been added to the **Shapes** window.

e. Choose **File→Shapes→Visio Extras→ Backgrounds (US units).**

2.	Add the **Logo** and the **Background solid** master to the drawing page.	a. In the **Backgrounds (US units)** stencil, select **Background solid** and apply it to the drawing page.
		b. Display the **Our Global Company** stencil.
		c. Drag the **Logo** master to the top-left corner of the drawing page.
		d. Resize the **Width** and **Height** of the **Logo** to *2 in*
		e. Position the **Logo** on the top-left corner of the drawing page.

3.	Add a watermark to the background.	a. Display the background page.
		b. On the **Standard** toolbar, select the **Text** tool.
		c. Drag the **Text** tool to create a rectangle in the center and type *OurGlobalCompany*
		d. Select the **Pointer** tool and click outside the rectangle to deselect it.
		e. Click the text **OurGlobalCompany,** and choose **Format**→**Text** to display the **Text** dialog box.
		f. From the **Size** drop-down list, select **48 pt** and click **OK.**
		g. If necessary, expand the text box to fit the text in a single line.
		h. In the **Size & Position** window, change the **Angle** of the text to *45* and press **Enter.**
		i. Display the **Text** dialog box.
		j. In the **General** section, in the **Transparency** text box, double-click and type *50*
		k. Click **Apply** and then click **OK.**
		l. Click away from the text box to deselect it.

4. Save the drawing as a template.

    a. Display **Page-1.**

    b. Observe the overall appearance of the drawing page.

    c. Choose **File→Save As.**

    d. In the **Save As** dialog box, navigate to the **C:\Program Files\Microsoft Office\ Templates** folder.

    e. In the **File name** text box, click and type *My Template*

    f. From the **Save as type** drop-down list, select **Template (*.vst)** and click **Save.**

    g. Close the drawing.

Lesson 3 Follow-up

In this lesson, you created custom styles and templates. Using custom styles and templates, you can maintain consistency across the documents you create.

1. **What do you think is the most convenient method for modifying the style of a shape and for applying similar formatting to the other shapes?**

2. **On your job, why do you think you would create a template?**

4 Designing a Floor Plan

Lesson Time: 45 minutes

Lesson Objectives:

In this lesson, you will design a floor plan.

You will:

● Create an office layout.

● Work with layers.

Introduction

You created a custom template to suit your needs. There are times when working on a drawing, you may need to edit certain aspects of it without affecting the rest. In this lesson, you will design a floor plan by assigning shapes to different layers.

You are working on the blueprint of a new project. As the project nears completion, a minor alteration is required to enhance the quality of the plan. However, you have to carry out the alteration after making sure that other components remain unchanged. You can simplify your task by assigning different components to different layers so that they remain independent of each other.

TOPIC A
Create an Office Layout

You created custom shapes and templates. You might use these shapes in a drawing to create a layout. Designing a layout will help you manage the space effectively. In this topic, you will create an office layout.

You are planning to build your own office. Your architect has suggested that you give a simple representation of what you desire to build a plan based on that. Visio provides tools that can be used to draw the basic layout of the each room.

The Drawing Scale

The *drawing scale* describes the ratio by which the real object has been magnified or shrunk. Drawings that contain scaled shapes are called *scaled drawings*. Most templates in Visio have predefined drawing scales; however, you can change the scale in any drawing. Each shape is designed to work with the template they come with, but can be modified and used in other templates too. When you drag a shape onto a drawing page, the shape resizes to match the drawing scale.

Ruler Zero Point

The location at which the X and Y coordinates intersect is called the *ruler zero point*. It is, by default, located at the bottom-left corner of the drawing page. The ruler zero point is used to measure the distance at which a shape is placed. However, this point can be relocated anywhere in the drawing page to suit your needs.

The Convert to Walls Command

The **Convert to Walls** command is used to convert shapes to walls, and allows you to specify the wall size and settings.

How to Create an Office Layout

Procedure Reference: Change the Drawing Scale

To change the drawing scale:

1. Display the drawing page for which you want to change the drawing scale.
2. Choose **File→Page Setup** to display the **Page Setup** dialog box.
3. In the **Page Setup** dialog box, select the **Drawing Scale** tab.
4. Change the drawing scale.
   - Select **Pre-defined scale** and from the drop-down list, select the desired drawing scale.
   - Or, select **Custom** and in the text box, specify the dimensions of the drawing scale.
5. Select the **Page Properties** tab and from the **Measurement units** drop-down list, select the desired measurement unit.
6. Click **Apply** and then click **OK** to save the changes and update the drawing page.

Procedure Reference: Reset the Ruler Zero Point

To reset the ruler zero point:

1. Display the drawing page for which you want to change the position of the ruler zero point.
2. Change the ruler zero point.
   - Change the ruler zero point of both the rulers.
     a. Place the mouse pointer at the intersection of the two rulers.
     b. Hold down **Ctrl** and drag to reposition the ruler zero point at the desired position.
   - Change the ruler zero point of any one ruler.
     a. Place the mouse pointer on the ruler whose zero point you want to modify.
     b. Hold down **Ctrl** and drag to reposition the ruler zero point at the desired position.

 To return the zero point to the bottom-left corner of the page, double-click the intersection of the two rulers.

Procedure Reference: Create an Office Layout

To create an office layout:

1. Choose **File→New→Maps and Floor Plans→Office Layout (US units)** to display the stencils related to creating an office layout.

2. From the displayed stencils, add the desired shape to the drawing page.

   • Use the **Cubicles (US units)** stencil to add workstations and storage units.

   • Use the **Office Accessories (US units)** stencil to add accessories such as plant, waste can, and paper tray.

   • Use the **Office Equipment (US units)** stencil to add equipments such as telephone, PC, and switch.

   • Use the **Office Furniture (US units)** stencil to add furniture such as tables, desks, and chairs.

   • Use the **Walls, Doors and Windows (US units)** stencil to add different shapes of rooms, doors, and windows.

3. If necessary, choose **Shape→Rotate or Flip→Rotate Right** to modify the shapes.

4. Use the **Size & Position** window to set the coordinates for the shapes at the desired location on the drawing page.

Convert to Walls

You can create walls by positioning shapes on the drawing page, uniting them by using the **Union** command, and then converting them to walls by using the **Convert to Walls** command from the **Plan** menu. In the **Convert to Walls** dialog box, the wall shape and the settings can be changed as needed.

ACTIVITY 4-1

Creating an Office Layout

Data Files:

Office Layout.vsd

Before You Begin:

From the C:\084902Data\Designing A Floor Plan folder, open the Office Layout.vsd file.

Scenario:

As an architect you need to help your client renovate his old office. You feel that one half of the building needs minor remodeling, while the other half has to be newly constructed. Your client provides you with the specifications for the new space to be constructed and also gives you the blueprint of the old plan. You start drawing a new layout based on the old plan.

What You Do	How You Do It
1. Modify the drawing scale and the location of the ruler zero point.	a. Choose **File→Page Setup** to display the **Page Setup** dialog box.
	b. Select the **Drawing Scale** tab.
	c. In the **Drawing scale** section, verify that in the **Pre-defined scale** drop-down list, **Architectural** is selected and in the second drop-down list, **1/2″ = 1' 0″** is selected.
	d. Select the **Page Properties** tab and from the **Measurement units** drop-down list, select **Feet (decimal).**
	e. Click **OK.**
	f. Hold down **Ctrl** and from the intersection of the two rulers, drag the four-headed arrow and drop it at the top-left corner of the drawing page.

g. Verify that the ruler zero point for both rulers starts from the top-left corner of the **Room** on the drawing page.

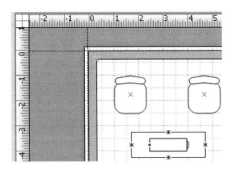

---

2. Add walls to the layout.

a. From the **Walls, Doors and Windows (US units)** stencil, drag the **Wall** master and using the status bar as an indicator, drop the master at **Begin X = 6 ft** and **Begin Y = -8 ft** on the drawing page.

b. In the **Size & Position** window, set the **Length** to *5 ft* and **Angle** to *90*

c. Using the status bar as an indicator, position the wall at **Begin X = 6 ft** and **Begin Y= -5.317 ft** on the drawing page.

d. Hold down **Ctrl** and drag an instance of the wall and place it next to the projection screen at **Begin X = 13.3 ft** and **Begin Y = -5.317 ft** on the drawing page.

e. Copy another instance of the wall next to the projection screen and place it at the center of the drawing page.

f. Choose **Shape→Rotate or Flip→Rotate Left.**

g. Move the endpoint of the wall and glue it to the room at both ends. Glue the wall to the endpoint of the two vertical walls.

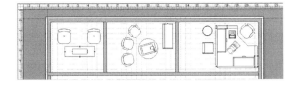

---

3. Add doors to the rooms.

a. From the **Walls, Doors and Windows (US units)** stencil, drag the **Door** master and drop it on the horizontal wall, below the table of the first room.

b. In the **Size & Position** window, set the **X** coordinate to *3.22 ft*

c. Change the **Width** to *1 ft*

d. Similarly, copy two more instances of the door to add it to the other two rooms.

e. From the **Walls, Doors and Windows (US units)** stencil, drag the **Double door** master to the center of the drawing page.

f. In the **Size & Position** window, set the **X** coordinate to *0.25 ft*

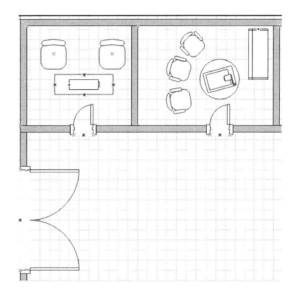

g. Verify that the **Width** is **60 in.**

h. If necessary, choose **Shape→Rotate or Flip→Flip Horizontal.**

4. Add switches to the rooms.

    a. From the **Office Equipment (US units)** stencil, drag the **Switch** master to the center of the drawing page.

    b. In the **Size & Position** window, set the **X** and **Y** coordinates to *2.5 ft* and *0 ft* respectively.

    c. Set the **Width** to *0.625 ft*

    d. Verify that **Height** changes to **1.25 ft.**

    e. If necessary, set the **Angle** to *-90*

    f. Similarly, copy two more instances of the switch to add it to the other two rooms.

5. Create the reception room.

a. From the **Cubicles (US units)** stencil, drag the **Straight workstation** master to the center of the drawing page.

b. In the **Size & Position** window, set the **X** coordinate to *18.8 ft* and verify that the **Y** coordinate is **-11 ft** and the **Width** and **Height** are **5 ft** and **7 ft,** respectively.

c. From the **Office Equipment (US units)** stencil, drag the **Telephone** master to the center of the drawing page.

d. In the **Size & Position** window, set the **X** and **Y** coordinates to *17.833 ft* and *-8.25 ft* respectively and verify that the **Width** and **Height** are **0 ft. 8 in** and **0 ft. 6 in,** respectively.

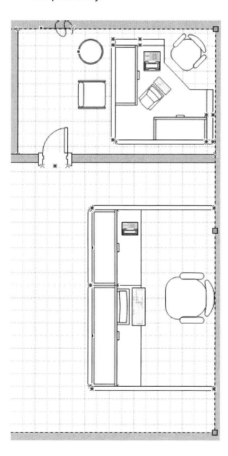

6. Enhance the reception room.

a. From the **Office Accessories (US units)** stencil, drag the **Large plant** master to the center of the drawing page.

b. In the **Size & Position** window, set the **X** and **Y** coordinates to *11 ft* and *-10.5 ft* respectively and verify that both the **Width** and **Height** are **3 ft.**

c. From the **Office Furniture (US units)** stencil, drag the **Swivel tilt chair** master to the center of the drawing page.

d. In the **Size & Position** window, set the **X** and **Y** coordinates to *11 ft* and *-14 ft* respectively and verify that both the **Width** and **Height** are **30 in** and set the **Angle** to *90*

e. Drag an instance of the **Sofa** and the **Table** masters to the center of the drawing page.

f. Select the sofa and choose **Shape→ Rotate or Flip→Rotate Left.**

g. Drag and place the sofa to the left of the swivel tilt chair.

h. In the **Size & Position** window, change the **Height** to *72 in*

i. Select the table and in the **Size & Position** window, set the **X** and **Y** coordinates to *6.75 ft* and *-11.375 ft* respectively and the **Width** and **Height** to *1.75 ft* and *4.5 ft* respectively and the **Angle** to *90*

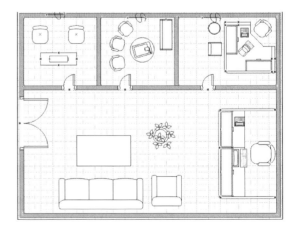

j. Save the file as *My Office Layout.vsd*

TOPIC B
Work with Layers

You have created an office layout in Visio. As your drawings get more complicated, you make sure that the changes you make to it don't affect the finalized shapes. In this topic, you will group shapes into different layers.

While building a card castle, you know that any minor disturbance would lead to a catastrophe. Similarly, while modifying an office layout it would be helpful to secure certain areas in the outline. This would provide scope to try changes with the other perspective of the layout and further, safeguarding the completed regions would save time spent on rework.

Layers

A *layer* is a named category that enables you to group related shapes on a drawing page. Layers can be predefined or custom. The properties of the layers can be modified using the **Layer Properties** dialog box, which can also be used to assign the selected shapes to the respective layer.

The Layer Properties Dialog Box

The **Layer Properties** dialog box displays the number of shapes assigned to each layer and controls the properties of the various shapes. The following table describes the various properties of the dialog box.

Property	*Description*
Visible	Specifies whether shapes on a layer are visible or hidden on the drawing page.
Print	Specifies whether shapes on a layer can be printed or not.
Active	Specifies whether shapes can be assigned to a layer.
Lock	Specifies whether a layer can be protected from being altered or selected.
Snap	Specifies whether shapes on a layer can snap to other shapes.
Glue	Specifies whether shapes on a layer can glue to other shapes.
Color	Specifies whether shapes on a layer appear in the specified color.

How to Work with Layers

Procedure Reference: Add a Layer

To add a layer:

1. Choose **View→Layer Properties** to display the **Layer Properties** dialog box.
2. In the **Layer Properties** dialog box, click **New** to display the **New Layer** dialog box.
3. In the **New Layer** dialog box, in the **Layer name** text box, type a name for the layer.
4. Click **OK** to display the **Layer Properties** dialog box.
5. Click **Apply** and then click **OK** to add a layer.

Procedure Reference: Assign Shapes to Layers

To assign shapes to layers:

1. Select the desired shape on the drawing page.
2. Choose **Format→Layer** to display the **Layer** dialog box.
3. In the **Layer** dialog box, in the **On layer(s)** section, check the desired check box to which you want to assign the shape.
4. Click **OK** to assign the selected shape to the layer.

Procedure Reference: Edit Layer Properties

To edit layer properties:

1. Select the desired shape on the drawing page.
2. Choose **View→Layer Properties** to display the **Layer Properties** dialog box.
3. Edit shapes in a layer using the **Layer Properties** dialog box.
   - Hide the desired shape from view.
     a. In the **Layer Properties** dialog box, uncheck the **Visible** check box in the desired layer.
     b. Click **Apply** and then click **OK** to hide the desired shape from view.
   - Rename the desired layer.
     a. In the **Layer Properties** dialog box, click **Rename** to display the **Rename Layer** dialog box.
     b. In the **Rename Layer** dialog box, in the **Layer name** text box, type a name for the layer.
     c. Click **Apply** and then click **OK** to rename the desired layer.
   - Activate a layer.
     a. In the **Layer Properties** dialog box, check the **Active** check box in the desired layer so that all shapes you add from then on are assigned to that specific layer.
     b. Click **Apply** and then click **OK** to activate the desired layer.
   - Lock a layer.
     a. In the **Layer Properties** dialog box, check the **Lock** check box for the desired layer so that none of the shapes in that layer can be selected or altered.
     b. Click **Apply** and then click **OK** to lock the desired layer.
   - Set a color for a layer.

a. In the **Layer Properties** dialog box, check the **Color** check box in the desired layer.
b. From the **Layer color** drop-down list, select the desired color.
c. Click **Apply** and then click **OK** to set the color for the selected layer.

ACTIVITY 4-2

Working with Layers

Data Files:

My Office Layout.vsd

Before You Begin:

The My Office Layout.vsd file is kept open.

Scenario:

Having almost executed the layout, you sit with your client for discussion. Your client wants you to show him a sketch, changing the workstations in the drawing without altering the position of the telephone, and also wants you to add color to the interiors.

What You Do	How You Do It
1. Add a new layer.	a. Choose **View→Layer Properties** to display the **Layer Properties** dialog box.
	b. In the **Layer Properties** dialog box, click **New** to display the **New Layer** dialog box.
	c. In the **New Layer** dialog box, in the **Layer name** text box, type *Telephone 1*
	d. Click **OK.**
	e. In the **Layer Properties** dialog box, click **Apply** and then click **OK** to add a new layer.
2. Assign shapes to the new layer.	a. On the drawing page, select the telephones.
	b. Choose **Format→Layer** to display the **Layer** dialog box.
	c. In the **Layer** dialog box, in the **On layer(s)** section, scroll down and check the **Telephone 1** check box and uncheck the rest.
	d. Click **OK** to assign the telephones to the **Telephone 1** layer.

3. Lock the **Telephone 1** layer.

    a. Choose **View→Layer Properties** to display the **Layer Properties** dialog box.

    b. In the **Layer Properties** dialog box, scroll down and check the **Lock** check box for the **Telephone 1** layer.

    c. Click **Apply** and then click **OK** to lock the layer.

    d. Click a telephone.

    e. Observe that it cannot be selected.

    f. Select the straight workstation.

    g. Delete it.

    h. Observe that the telephone is not deleted.

    i. On the **Standard** toolbar, click the **Undo** button.

4. Color the furniture in the layout.

    a. Choose **View→Layer Properties** to display the **Layer Properties** dialog box.

    b. In the **Layer Properties** dialog box, check the **Color** check box for the **Furniture** layer.

    c. In the **Layer color** drop-down list, scroll up and select **02:.**

    d. Check the **Color** check box for the **Movable Furnishings** layer.

    e. In the **Layer color** drop-down list, scroll up and select **02:.**

    f. Click **Apply** and then click **OK** to add color.

    g. Close the **Size & Position** window.

    h. Save and close the file.

Lesson 4 Follow-up

In this lesson, you designed a floor plan using layers. By creating a layout, you assigned shapes to various layers and changed the properties of the various shapes.

1. **On the job, how beneficial is the drawing scale?**

2. **How do you think you will use layers to benefit your drawing?**

5 Representing External Data in Visio

Lesson Time: 1 hour(s)

Lesson Objectives:

In this lesson, you will represent external data in Visio.

You will:

- Generate a PivotDiagram.
- Create an organization chart using external data.
- Import project plan data into Visio.
- Link to a database.
- Import Excel data.

Introduction

You have designed an office layout. However, the data you want to represent may not always be in a format that you require. In this lesson, you will represent external data in Visio.

While working with a team, different team members may be comfortable with different software applications. Thus, while coordinating with your colleagues, you may need to deal with data saved in different file formats. Rather than reworking the data you have, integrating them with Visio would save time as well as help avoid potential errors.

TOPIC A
Generate a PivotDiagram

You have added shape data to your shapes manually using the data available. While working in a team, your colleague may give you a workbook with all the necessary data. In this topic, you will generate a PivotDiagram using the given data.

You are working on a high priority project and are expecting some details from your colleague. As your colleague is in a hurry too, she drops off the data as an Access database. While trying to represent the data in your drawing, you unknowingly leave out a section of the table. Although a small error, reworking on it would be a tedious task. Visio enables you to automatically import data as PivotDiagrams, thus saving the time you would spend on rework.

PivotDiagrams

A *PivotDiagram* is a hierarchical representation of shapes. This structure enables you to analyze and summarize complex data into easily comprehendible visual formats. The PivotDiagram starts out as a single shape called the *top node* that contains imported information. Along with the top node, the details of the source data, the *data legend* is added to the drawing page. In Visio, the **PivotDiagram** template enables you to represent data from various sources like Excel, Access, SQL Server, and others.

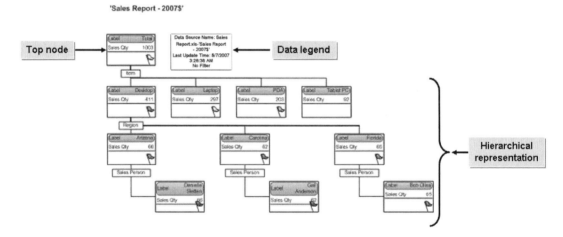

Figure 5-1: A PivotDiagram.

 Each rectangular shape in a PivotDiagram is called a Pivot node.

Data Graphics

Data graphic is an enhancement feature that enables you to define the appearance of the data in your drawing. A data graphic may be a combination of textual and graphical representation of the data. They can be used to represent different types of data such as region, sales, and employee. In Visio, you can access the data graphics via the **Data Graphics** task pane. This feature enables you to add text to shapes, add data bars and icons to represent values, and even color them based on unique values or a range of values.

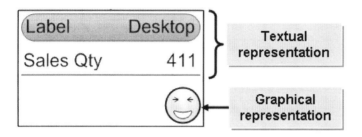

Figure 5-2: *The different types of data graphics.*

 A data graphic can be used to enhance shapes in all types of drawings irrespective of the shape used in the drawing. To use a data graphic, you must however, define the shape data of the shape.

The PivotDiagram Window

The **PivotDiagram** window is displayed after data is imported into a PivotDiagram. This window enables you to choose the data field that is to be represented in the drawing.

Section	Description
Add Category	Displays the categories based on which the source data is to be grouped. The categories displayed in this section correspond to the columns in the source data. This section enables you to break the selected node into sub nodes based on category names, select all nodes that are broken into categories, edit the appearance of the data, and configure column.
Add Total	Displays the columns in the source data that can be summarized and listed in the nodes. This section enables you to sum up the values, determine the average, calculate the maximum and minimum values, and indicate the number of rows contained in each node.

Section	Description
Actions	Enables you to enhance the PivotDiagram by adding shapes, refreshing data, sorting, editing the data graphics, and rearranging the layout.

 The **Configure Column** displays the **Configure Column** dialog box that enables you to filter the rows of the source data to a subset that meets your requirements.

How to Generate a PivotDiagram

Procedure Reference: Create a PivotDiagram Using an Excel Workbook

To create a PivotDiagram using an Excel workbook:

1. Display the **Data Selector** wizard.
    *   In the **Getting Started** window, from the **Business** category, select **PivotDiagram (US units).**
    *   Choose **File→New→Business→PivotDiagram (US units).**
    *   Or, choose **Data→Insert PivotDiagram.**

 Apart from Excel workbooks, you can also import Access databases, Sharepoint Services list, SQL Server databases, SQL Services Analysis Services, and other OLEDB or ODBC data sources using the **Data Selector** wizard.

2. In the **Data Selector** wizard, on the **What data do you want to use** page, select **Microsoft Office Excel workbook** and click **Next.**
3. On the **What workbook do you want to import** page, navigate to the location of the source file and click **Next.**
4. On the **What worksheet or range do you want to use** page, specify the worksheet or range and click **Next.**
5. If necessary, on the **Connect to data** page, specify the rows and columns to be included.
6. Click **Next** and click **Finish** to import the data.
7. Click the top node and in the **Pivot Diagram** window, in the **Add Category** section, select the desired category to group the data.

Procedure Reference: Edit a PivotDiagram

To edit a PivotDiagram:

1. If necessary, open the desired PivotDiagram.
2. Click the top node and in the **PivotDiagram** window, in the **Add Category** section, select the desired category to group the data.
3. Change how the numeric data is displayed using the **Add Total** section.
    *   Check or uncheck the desired field to show or hide the corresponding values.
    *   Right-click the item you want to change and choose the desired summary function.

4. If necessary, format the shape further.

    a. In the **Actions** section, click **Apply Shape.**

    b. In the **Apply Shape** dialog box, from the **Stencil** drop-down list, select the desired stencil.

    c. Select the desired shape and click **OK.**

Procedure Reference: Add Data Graphics to Shapes

To add data graphics to shapes:

1. Choose **Data→Display Data on Shapes** to display the **Data Graphics** task pane.

2. If necessary, select the shape to which you want to apply the data graphic.

3. In the **Data Graphics** task pane, right-click the data graphic you want to add to your text and choose **Edit Data Graphic** to display the **Edit Data Graphic** dialog box.

4. Add text to the data graphic.

    a. From the **New Item** drop-down list, select **Text.**

    b. In the **New Text** dialog box, from the **Data field** drop-down list, select the desired item as the field.

    c. From the **Callout** drop-down list, select the desired style for the callout.

    d. If necessary, uncheck the **Use default position** check box to modify the **Horizontal** and **Vertical** positions of the callout.

    e. In the **Details** section, modify the properties to determine how the text data will appear.

    f. Click **OK.**

5. Add a data bar to the data graphic.

    a. From the **New Item** drop-down list, select **Data Bar.**

    b. In the **New Data Bar** dialog box, from the **Data Field** drop-down list, select the desired item as the field.

    c. From the **Callout** drop-down list, select the desired style for the callout.

    d. If necessary, uncheck the **Use default position** check box to modify the **Horizontal** and **Vertical** positions of the callout.

    e. In the **Details** section, modify the properties to determine how the data bar will appear.

    f. Click **OK.**

6. Add an icon to the data graphic.

    a. From the **New Item** drop-down list, select **Icon Set.**

    b. In the **New Icon Set** dialog box, from the **Data Field** drop-down list, select the desired item as the field.

    c. From the **Callout** drop-down list, select the desired style for the icon set.

    d. If necessary, check the **Use default position** check box to use the default **Horizontal** and **Vertical** positions of the callout.

    e. In the **Rules for showing each icon** section, modify the values to determine how the icons will represent the data.

    f. Click **OK.**

7. Add color to the data graphic based on values.

   a. From the **New Item** drop-down list, select **Color by Value.**

   b. In the **New Color by Value** dialog box, from the **Data field** drop-down list, select the desired item as the field.

   c. From the **Coloring method** drop-down list, select the desired option to set the color accordingly.

   d. In the **Color assignments** section, set the desired value or range of values, fill color, and text color.

   e. If necessary, insert or delete field values.

   f. Click **OK.**

8. In the **Edit Data Graphic** dialog box, verify that the new data graphic is added and click **Apply** and then click **OK.**

 You can directly remove the data graphics from a shape by right-clicking the shape and choosing **Data→Remove Data Graphic.**

Edit a Data Graphic

If you want to modify the attributes of a data graphic, you can do so without redoing the entire formatting. However, it is better to duplicate the master copy and then make changes to it. To edit the data graphic, in the **Edit Data Graphic** dialog box, select the desired data field and click **Edit Item** to edit the selected item field. In case you want to delete a data graphic, right-click the data graphic and choose **Delete.**

ACTIVITY 5-1

Generating a PivotDiagram

Data Files:

Sales Report.xlsx, Custom Template.vst

Before You Begin:

Display the **Getting Started** window.

Scenario:

The sales team in your organization has done an exceptional sale of desktops this quarter. Your manager has asked you to create a chart with the sale details. She has provided you with an Excel workbook for the same. Rather than re-creating the workbook, you decide to import the data into a PivotDiagram.

What You Do	How You Do It
1. Import the Excel workbook as a PivotDiagram.	a. In the **Getting Started** window, from the **Business** templates, select **PivotDiagram** and click **Create.**
	b. In the **Data Selector** wizard, on the **What data do you want to use** page, verify that **Microsoft Office Excel workbook** is selected and click **Next.**
	c. On the **What workbook do you want to import** page, click **Browse.**
	d. In the **Data Selector** dialog box, navigate to the **C:\084902Data\Representing External Data** folder, and open the Sales Report.xlsx file.
	e. Click **Next** three times.

 On the **What worksheet or range do you want to use** page, the worksheet that is to be imported is displayed. After selecting the desired worksheet, on the **Connect to data** page, you can specify the columns and rows that you wish to import or select all the columns and rows. Once you have specified the rows and columns to be imported, click **Finish** to complete the importing.

		f.	Click **Finish** to import the worksheet.
2.	Add the **Item** category as a sub-node.	a.	Zoom the drawing page to **100%** to clearly view the top node and the data legend.
		b.	If necessary, scroll to display the top node.
		c.	Verify that the top node is selected.
		d.	In the **PivotDiagram** window, in the **Add Category** section, right-click **Item** and choose **Add Item.**
		e.	Observe that the items have been added as sub-nodes to the top node.
3.	Add the other categories as a sub-node to the **Desktop** node.	a.	Select the **Desktop** node.
		b.	In the **Add Category** section, place the mouse pointer over the **Region** category and from the **Region** drop-down list, select **Add Region.**
		c.	On the **PivotDiagram** toolbar, click the **Layout Direction** button, ⊞ and choose **Left-to-Right.**
		d.	Add the **Sales Person** category.
4.	Display the average of the sales quantity.	a.	Click anywhere to deselect the shapes.
		b.	In the **Add Total** section, in the **Sales Qty(Sum)** drop-down list, verify that only **Sum** is selected and select **Avg.**
		c.	On the drawing page, observe that the average sale value has been added to each node.

5. Format the drawing using data graphics.

   a. Choose **Data→Display Data on Shapes.**

   b. In the **Data Graphics** task pane, in the **Apply a data graphic** section, right-click the second icon and choose **Duplicate.**

   c. Right-click the newly duplicated data graphic, **Data Graphic.10** and choose **Edit Data Graphic.**

   d. In the **Edit Data Graphic** dialog box, verify that the first field is selected and click **Edit Item.**

   e. In the **Edit Text** dialog box, from the **Callout** drop-down list, select **Bubble callout** and click **OK.**

6. Add a new icon to represent the sale quantity.

a. In the **Edit Data Graphic** dialog box, click **New Item** and choose **Icon Set**.

b. In the **New Icon Set** dialog box, from the **Data field** drop-down list, select **Sales Qty(Avg).**

c. From the **Callout** drop-down list, select the third option to represent the sale quantity as flags.

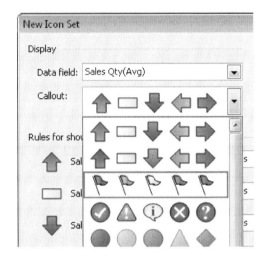

d. In the **Callout position** section, from the **Horizontal** drop-down list, select **Center** and from the **Vertical** drop-down list, select **Bottom.**

e. In the **Rules for showing each icon** section, for the first row, set the value as **is greater than** and type *60*

f. For the second row, set the value as **is between** and press **Tab.**

g. Type *21* and press **Tab.** Then type *40*

h. For the third row, set the value as **is between** and set the range as *41* and *60*

i. Click **OK.**

j. Click **Apply** and then click **OK.**

7. Apply the data graphic to all the shapes.

a. Select all the shapes.

b. Right-click the newly modified data graphic icon and choose **Apply to Selected Shapes.**

c. Observe that the data graphics have been updated.

d. Save the file as *My Sales Report.vsd* and close it.

TOPIC B

Create an Organization Chart from External Data

You created organizational charts by dragging shapes onto the drawing page. However, most organizations usually have their organization's information documented, which can be used to create an organizational chart in Visio. In this topic, you will use the external data to create an organizational chart.

You have been asked to present the newly joined employees with an orientation program. Apart from the other things that need to be covered, you will have to describe the organizational structure to them. Your colleague has given you a worksheet that describes the various teams in the organization. Though accurate, an hierarchal representation of the organization structure would mean better comprehension. However, reworking on the data you have is a tiresome task. Visio enables you to import data into an organization chart.

Hyperlinks

A *hyperlink* is a link that acts as a connection across documents or between two sections of a single document. The link is represented by a globe-like icon, which is displayed when you place the mouse pointer over a linked shape. The **Organization Chart Wizard** enables you to automatically link content across different pages in the drawing.

 In Visio, a hyperlink can be added to another page or shape with the same attribute, a page or shape in another drawing, or to external information. Shapes with different attributes are hard to link.

How to Create an Organization Chart from External Data

Procedure Reference: Create an Organization Chart from External Data

To create an organization chart from external data:

1. Display the **Organization Chart Wizard.**

    *   In the **Getting Started** window, in the **Business** category, select **Organization Chart Wizard (US Units).**

    *   Choose **File→New→Business→Organization Chart Wizard (US Units).**

    *   Or, choose **Data→Insert Data Solutions→Organization Chart.**

2. In the **Organization Chart Wizard,** on the **I want to create my organization chart from** page, select the desired information source and click **Next.**

3. On the **My organization information is stored in** page, select the format in which the source data is stored in and click **Next.**

4. On the **Locate the file that contains your organization information** page, click **Browse,** navigate to and select the source file, and click **Next.**

5. On the **Choose the columns (fields) in your data file that contain the information that defines the organization** page, set the necessary field data and click **Next.**

6. On the **Choose the columns (fields) from your data file that you want to display** page, select the desired columns and add them to the displayed fields.

7. Click **Next.**

8. On the **Choose the columns (fields) from your data file that you want to add to organization chart shapes as shape data fields** page, add the desired columns and click **Next.**

9. Click **Finish** to create an organization chart from external data.

Procedure Reference: Add a Hyperlink to External Sources

To add a hyperlink to external sources:

1. Open the desired drawing.

2. Select the desired shape.

3. Choose **Insert→Hyperlinks.**

4. Using the **Hyperlinks** dialog box, insert the hyperlink.

   a. In the **Address** text box, enter the location of the file.

   b. If necessary, add the description that would be displayed when you place the mouse pointer over the hyperlink.

   c. If necessary, click **New** to insert a new hyperlink to the same shape.

   d. If necessary, uncheck the **Use relative path for hyperlink** check box, to use the relative path that describes the location of the linked file in relation to your Visio drawing.

5. Click **OK.**

Procedure Reference: Link to Different Pages in a Drawing

To link to different pages in a drawing:

1. Open the desired drawing.

2. Choose **Insert→Hyperlinks.**

3. In the **Hyperlinks** dialog box, click the **Browse** button adjacent to the **Sub - address** text box.

4. In the **Hyperlink** dialog box, select the page and shape you want to link.

5. Click **OK.**

6. If necessary, add a description.

7. Click **OK.**

ACTIVITY 5-2

Creating an Organization Chart from Excel Workbook

Data Files:

Organization Chart Data.xlsx

Before You Begin:

Display the **Getting Started** window.

Scenario:

You are the HR executive in your organization. There has been restructuring in your organization recently. You have an Excel workbook containing the recent updates. You wish to draw an organization chart using this workbook.

What You Do	How You Do It
1. Display the **Organization Chart Wizard.**	a. In the **Getting Started** window, in the **Template Categories** task pane, click the **Business** link.
	b. In the **Business** task pane, scroll down and select **Organization Chart Wizard,** and click **Create.**

2. Import the Excel workbook.

a. In the **Organization Chart Wizard,** on the **I want to create my organization chart from** page, verify that **Information that's already stored in a file or database** is selected and click **Next.**

b. On the **My organization information is stored in** page, verify that **A text, Org Plus (*.txt), or Excel file** is selected and click **Next.**

c. On the **Locate the file that contains your organization information** page, click **Browse.**

d. In the **Organization Chart Wizard** dialog box, navigate to the **C:\084902Data\ Representing External Data** folder, and open the Organization Chart Data.xlsx file.

e. In the **Organization Chart Wizard,** click **Next.**

f. On the **Choose the columns (fields) in your data file that contain the information that defines the organization** page, from the **Reports to** drop-down list, select **Supervised by** and click **Next.**

g. On the **Choose the columns (fields) from your data file that you want to display** page, in the **Data file columns** list box, hold down **Shift** and click **Department** to select both the options, and click **Add.**

h. Click **Next.**

i. On the **Choose the columns (fields) from your data file that you want to add to the organization chart shapes as shape data fields** page, hold down **Shift** and click **Department** to select the four options and then click **Add.**

j. Click **Next.**

k. Verify that **Hyperlink employee shapes across pages** is checked and click **Finish.**

3.	Format the chart to fit the drawing page.	a.	Display **Page-1**.
		b.	Display the **Page Setup** dialog box.
		c.	In the **Page Setup** dialog box, on the **Print Setup** tab, in the **Printer paper** drop-down list, scroll down and select **Ledger (B): 17 in. x 11 in.**
		d.	Click **Apply** and then click **OK.**
		e.	Select all the shapes and position them in the center of the drawing page.
		f.	Zoom the page to **75%** to view the chart clearly.
4.	Test the hyperlinks.	a.	If necessary, scroll down to display the end of the organization chart.
		b.	Click away to deselect the shapes.
		c.	Right-click the shape and choose **Page-3/ Sheet.1.**
		d.	Zoom the page **100%.**
		e.	Observe that the shape has been linked to a shape with the same attribute.
		f.	Save the file as ***My Organization Chart.vsd*** and close it.

TOPIC C
Import Project Plan Data into Visio

You have created an organizational chart. Sometimes, you may want to display your project plan to your team members. In this topic, you will import project plan data into Visio.

You are to give a presentation to your clients regarding your new project. As you look into the project plan, you find that it is very mundane, with numerous rows and columns of statistical information. In order to sustain the interest of your audience, you decide to represent the project data visually using Visio.

The Gantt Chart

A *Gantt chart* is a graphical representation of statistical information in the form of bar graphs. This chart is generally used in project management and helps plan, coordinate, and track specific tasks in a project. The horizontal axis on the Gantt chart represents time period and the vertical axis represents the different tasks.

Timelines

A *timeline* is a linear representation of a specific time period and the tasks that occur during that time period. Generally, timelines are used to represent the project's current status, history of events, and the upcoming tasks.

 A project plan may include one or more timelines that can be synchronized.

How to Import Project Plan Data into Visio

Procedure Reference: Import Project Data as a Gantt Chart

To import project data as a Gantt chart:

1. Display the **Import Project Data Wizard.**
   - Choose **Data→Insert Data Solutions→Gantt Chart.**
   - Or, display the wizard using the **Gantt Chart** menu.
     a. In the **Getting Started** window, choose **Schedule→Gantt Chart.**
     b. In the **Gantt Chart Options** dialog box, click **Cancel.**
     c. Choose **Gantt Chart→Import.**

2. On the **I want to create my project schedule from** page, select the desired option and click **Next.**

 This procedure is written with reference to the **Information that's already stored in a file** option.

3. On the **Select the format of your project data** page, select the file format of the source file and click **Next.**

4. On the **Select the file containing existing project schedule data** page, click **Browse,** navigate to and open the desired source file, and then click **Next.**

5. On the **Time scale** page, set the desired units and duration options and then click **Next.**

6. On the **Select task types to include** page, select the desired task and click **Next.**

7. Click **Finish** to import the file.

Procedure Reference: Import Project Data as a Timeline

To import project data as a timeline:

 To import project data as a timeline, you would require the **Microsoft Office Project** application installed on your system.

1. Open a new drawing.

2. Choose **Data→Insert Data Solutions→Timeline** to display the **Import Timeline Wizard.**

3. In the **Import Timeline Wizard,** navigate to and select the source file.

4. Click **Next.**

5. On the **Select task types to include** page, select the desired task type and click **Next.**

6. On the **Select shapes for your Visio timeline** page, if necessary, select different shapes and click **Next.**

7. Click **Finish** to import the project plan data.

ACTIVITY 5-3

Importing Project Plan Data as a Gantt Chart

Data Files:

CSS Project Plan.xlsx

Before You Begin:

Display the **Getting Started** window.

Scenario:

You have worked on the CSS project. A new member has joined your team. You have been asked to assist him in the project. So rather than giving him statistical data, you decide to show him a chart of the project plan.

What You Do	How You Do It
1. Display the **Import Project Data Wizard.**	a. In the **Getting Started** window, in the **Template Categories** task pane, click the **Schedule** link.
	b. In the **Schedule** task pane, double-click **Gantt Chart.**
	c. In the **Gantt Chart Options** dialog box, click **Cancel.**
	d. Choose **Gantt Chart→Import.**

<table>
<tr>
<td>2.</td>
<td>Import the project plan into Visio.</td>
<td>a.</td>
<td>In the **Import Project Data Wizard,** verify that the **Information that's already stored in a file** option is selected and click **Next.**</td>
</tr>
<tr>
<td></td>
<td></td>
<td>b.</td>
<td>On the **Select the format of your project data** page, verify that **Microsoft Office Excel File** is selected and click **Next.**</td>
</tr>
<tr>
<td></td>
<td></td>
<td>c.</td>
<td>On the **Select the file containing existing project schedule data** page, click **Browse.**</td>
</tr>
<tr>
<td></td>
<td></td>
<td>d.</td>
<td>In the **Import Project Data Wizard** dialog box, navigate to the **C:\084902Data\ Representing External Data** folder and open the CSS Project Plan.xlsx file.</td>
</tr>
<tr>
<td></td>
<td></td>
<td>e.</td>
<td>Click **Next.**</td>
</tr>
<tr>
<td></td>
<td></td>
<td>f.</td>
<td>On the **Time scale** page, click **Next.**</td>
</tr>
<tr>
<td></td>
<td></td>
<td>g.</td>
<td>On the **Select task types to include** page, verify that **All** is selected and click **Next.**</td>
</tr>
<tr>
<td></td>
<td></td>
<td>h.</td>
<td>Click **Finish.**</td>
</tr>
<tr>
<td></td>
<td></td>
<td>i.</td>
<td>Observe that the project plan data is imported.</td>
</tr>
<tr>
<td>3.</td>
<td>View the different phases of the project.</td>
<td>a.</td>
<td>Zoom the chart to **80%.**</td>
</tr>
<tr>
<td></td>
<td></td>
<td>b.</td>
<td>Observe the different phases of the project plan.</td>
</tr>
<tr>
<td></td>
<td></td>
<td>c.</td>
<td>Save the file as *My Project Plan.vsd* and close it.</td>
</tr>
</table>

TOPIC D
Link to a Database

You have imported the project plan data into Visio. Linking the imported data directly to shapes, enables you to monitor each shape individually. In this topic, you will link shapes to a database.

While creating a network drawing, it is important to keep the updating shapes as changes are made to it. Linking a database to a shape, helps ensure that you can specifically edit the shape individually.

Databases

A *database* is a collection of data that is logically related and organized so that a computer program can access the desired information quickly. The data contained in a database can be textual, numeric, or graphical. The data in the database can be searched, retrieved, and manipulated.

How to Link to a Database

Procedure Reference: Link to a Database

To link to a database:

1. Open the file that contains the shapes to be linked.
2. Choose **Data→Link Data to Shapes.**
3. In the **Data Selector** dialog box, select **Microsoft Office Access database** and click **Next.**
4. On the **Connect to Microsoft Office Access Database** page, click **Browse** and navigate to the desired access file.
5. Click **Open** and then click **Next.**
6. Click **Next.**
7. Click **Finish.**
8. Observe that a pane opens up at the bottom of the file with the data in it.
9. Drag and drop the details from the lower pane on to the desired shape.
10. Observe that the data now appears against the shape.
11. If necessary, right-click the shape to which the data has been added, and then choose **Properties** to display the details of the linked shape.

ACTIVITY 5-4

Linking to a Database

Data Files:

Network.vsd, Network.accdb

Before You Begin:

From the C:\084902Data\Representing External Data folder, open the Network.vsd file.

Scenario:

The layout of your office has been changed. Using that layout drawing, you have added shapes to specify the location of the various networking components of your office. Your colleague from the IT department has given you an Access database with information about the various network components. You can now use this database in your drawing.

What You Do	How You Do It
1. Open the Network.vsd file.	a. Choose **Data→Link Data to Shapes.**
	b. In the **Data Selector** dialog box, select **Microsoft Office Access database** and click **Next.**
	c. On the **Connect to Microsoft Office Access Database** page, click **Browse** and navigate to the Network.accdb file.
	d. Click **Open** and then click **Next.**
	e. Click **Next.**
	f. Click **Finish.**
2. Link the shapes in the drawing to the database.	a. Observe that a pane opens up at the bottom of the file with the data in it.
	b. Drag and drop the details from the lower pane on to the desired shape.
	c. Observe that the data now appears against the shape.

3. View the linked content.

    a. Right-click the shape to which the data has been added, and then choose **Properties** to display the details of the linked shape.

    b. Save the changes to the Network.vsd file and close it.

TOPIC E
Import Excel Data

You linked a database to Visio. Sometimes, you may have to manually create a drawing with the given data. In this topic, you will manually import Excel data.

Automatically importing data may be an easy way to insert mapped content into Visio. However, there maybe times when specific data needs to be mapped to unique shapes. You can import data such that shapes are automatically linked, but manually linking the shapes to data would help monitor the link created between the shape and its corresponding data.

The External Data Window

The **External Data** window is displayed when you import data using the **Link Data to Shapes** command. This window displays the content of the source file that is to be linked to the shapes. Dragging the data from the **External Data** window to the shape links the data to the shape. Once data is linked to the shape, a link icon appears to the left of the window.

The Data Refresh Feature

While importing content into another application, a link is retained between the source file and the destination file. The changes made in the source file need to be implemented in the destination file. The data refresh feature in Visio enables you to refresh data manually or automatically at regular intervals. Imported data can be refreshed using the **Refresh Data** dialog box.

How to Import Excel Data
Procedure Reference: Import Excel Data

To import Excel data:

1. Open a new drawing.
2. Choose **Data→Link Data to Shapes** to display the **Data Selector** wizard.
3. In the **Data Selector** wizard, on the **What data do you want to use** page, verify that **Microsoft Office Excel workbook** is selected and click **Next.**
4. On the **What workbook do you want to import** page, click **Browse,** navigate to the desired source file, and click **Next.**
5. On the **What worksheet or range do you want to use** page, select the desired worksheet and click **Next.**
6. On the **Select the columns and rows to include** page, if necessary, select the desired columns and rows and click **Next.**
7. On the **Configure Refresh Unique Identifier** page, select the rows you wish to insert and click **Next.**
8. Click **Finish** to import the Excel data.

Procedure Reference: Link Imported Data Automatically

To link imported data automatically:

1. Open the desired drawing page.

2. Place the shapes on the drawing page.

3. Add shape data to the drawing page, to match content to the source data.

4. Import the source data using the **Link Data to Shapes** command.

5. Choose **Data→Automatically Link** to display the **Automatic Link** wizard.

6. In the **Automatic Link** wizard, on the **Automatically link rows to shapes** page, select the desired shape.

7. Click **Next.**

8. On the **Automatically link row to shape if** page, map the **Data Column** to the corresponding **Shape Field.**

9. If necessary, click **and** to map another data column to the source field.

10. Click **Next** and click **Finish** to link the data.

Procedure Reference: Link Imported Data Manually

To link imported data manually:

1. Open the desired drawing page.

2. Import the source data using the **Link Data to Shapes** command.

3. If necessary, choose **View→External Data Window** to display the **External Data** window.

4. Link data to shapes.

   - Drag a row from the **External Data** window onto a shape in the drawing to link rows to existing shapes.

   - Create shapes from your data.

     a. Click a master shape in the **Shapes** window.

     b. Drag a row or a set of rows from the **External Data** window onto the blank drawing page.

     c. Verify that the instance of the shape that is selected is added to the drawing page.

5. If necessary, add data graphics.

Procedure Reference: Refresh Imported Data in a Drawing

To refresh imported data in a drawing:

1. Open the desired drawing.

2. Choose **Data→Refresh Data** to display the **Refresh Data** dialog box.

> The **Refresh Data** option will be unavailable if you import data without using the data link features.

3. Using the **Refresh Data** dialog box, refresh the data.

   - Select the desired data source and then click **Refresh.**

   - Select **Refresh All** to refresh all source content simultaneously.

   - Set Visio to refresh data automatically.

     a. Check the **Show this dialog box on file open** check box and click **Configure.**

b. In the **Configure Refresh** dialog box, in the **Automatic Refresh** section, check the **Refresh every** check box.

c. In the **Refresh every** text box, set the desired time span.

d. If necessary, modify the **Unique Identifier.**

e. Click **OK.**

4. Click **Close.**

Refresh Data in PivotDiagrams

In a PivotDiagram, the **Refresh Data** option on the **Data** menu would be unavailable. Hence, to refresh data in a PivotDiagram, choose **PivotDiagram→Refresh Data.**

Resolve Conflicts

While refreshing data, sometimes, Visio may not be able to match the current shape with the new data. In such instances, the **Refresh Conflicts** task pane is displayed.

Procedure Reference: Add New Shape Data Property

To add new shape data property:

1. Display the **Define Shape Data** dialog box.

- Use the **Action** toolbar.

 a. On the **Action** toolbar, click the **Shape Data** button.

 b. In the **Shape Data** dialog box, click **Define.**

- Or, use the **Shape Data** window.

 a. Choose **View→Shape Data Window.**

 b. In the **Shape Data** window, right-click and choose **Define Shape Data.**

2. In the **Define Shape Data** dialog box, click **New** to create a new shape data property.

3. Enter the **Label** for the new property.

4. If necessary, change the other fields for the property.

5. Click **OK.**

ACTIVITY 5-5

Importing Excel Data into Visio

Data Files:

Work Flow.vsd, Employee Info.xlsx

Before You Begin:

1. From the C:\084902Data\Representing External Data folder, open the Work Flow.vsd file.
2. Close the **Shapes** window.

Scenario:

You are to give a presentation to the products team regarding the new workflow you wish to suggest. For this, you have created a basic workflow diagram. You have an Excel workbook with details about the employees of your organization. You decide to represent the employee information in the workflow drawing to add more value to it.

What You Do	How You Do It
1. Import the Excel workbook into Visio.	a. Choose **Data→Link Data to Shapes.**
	b. In the **Data Selector** wizard, verify that **Microsoft Office Excel workbook** is selected and click **Next.**
	c. On the **What workbook do you want to import** page, click **Browse.**
	d. In the **Data Selector** dialog box, navigate to the **C:\084902Data\Representing External Data** folder and open the Employee Info.xlsx file.
	e. Click **Next.**
	f. On the **What worksheet or range do you want to use** page, click **Next.**
	g. On the **Connect to data** page, click **Next** to include all rows and columns to the drawing.
	h. On the **Configure Refresh Unique Identifier** page, observe that **Employee ID (Recommended)** is selected as the unique identifier and click **Next.**
	i. Click **Finish** to import the Excel workbook.

2. Link data manually using the **External Data** window.

   a. Observe that the **External Data** window is displayed as soon as you finish importing data.

   b. In the **External Data** window, select the third row with the employee ID **1003** and then drag and drop it on the second shape on the left side of the drawing page.

   c. In the **External Data** window, observe that a link symbol is seen near the left corner of the third row.

⊖ 1003	Christophe...	research an...	Yves St.Pierre	Development

3. Link data automatically.

   a. Choose **Data→Automatically Link.**

   b. In the **Automatic Link - Sheet1** wizard, verify that **All shapes on this page** is selected and then click **Next.**

   c. On the **Automatically link row to shape if** page, click **Next** to map shapes with data that contain the same employee ID.

   d. Click **Finish.**

   e. In the **External Data** window, observe that a link is displayed to show that data is linked to the shape.

4.	Apply data graphics.	a. If necessary, choose **Data→Display Data on Shapes.**
		b. In the **Data Graphics** task pane, right-click the second icon, **Data Graphic** and choose **Duplicate.**
		c. Right-click the duplicated icon, **Data Graphic.30** and choose **Edit Data Graphic.**
		d. In the **Edit Data Graphic** dialog box, from the **New Item** drop-down list, select **Text.**
		e. In the **New Text** dialog box, from the **Data field** drop-down list, select **Name.**
		f. From the **Callout** drop-down list, select **Bubble callout** and click **OK.**
		g. Click **Apply** and then **OK.**
		h. Select all the shapes.
		i. Right-click the duplicated data graphic and select **Apply to Selected Shapes.**
5.	Set data to refresh regularly.	a. Choose **Data→Refresh Data.**
		b. In the **Refresh Data** dialog box, check the **Show this dialog box on file open** check box.
		c. Click **Configure.**
		d. In the **Configure Refresh** dialog box, in the **Automatic Refresh** section, check the **Refresh every** check box.
		e. In the **Refresh every** text box, type *30* and click **OK.**
		f. Click **Close.**
		g. Save the file as *My Work Flow.vsd* and close it.

Lesson 5 Follow-up

In this lesson, you represented external data in Visio. Importing data saved in other file formats into Visio, helps you save time and increase your efficiency.

1. **On a regular basis, what kind of files do you think you would import into Visio?**

2. **How do you think you will use the data graphics in your drawings?**

6 | Sharing Your Work

Lesson Time: 35 minutes

Lesson Objectives:

In this lesson, you will share your drawings.

You will:

● Link a Visio drawing to other applications.

● Convert a Visio drawing to a web page.

● Print a Visio drawing.

Introduction

You have created a layout with various shapes. Sometimes, you might want to share your work with your team, so that you can work in collaboration. In this lesson, you will share your drawing with others.

You may be part of a team that works from diverse locations on a common project. Each member of the team might not use the same application and might need to share work. Collaborating and working under such circumstances might be very tedious. Visio offers features that would let you collaborate in your work.

TOPIC A

Link a Visio Drawing to Other Applications

You have created custom stencils and shapes. You want to share your drawings with co-workers who don't have Visio installed on their computers. In this topic, you will link a Visio drawing to other applications.

Your organization has teamed up with another company for a new project. You now need to ensure that members from the new company work in collaboration with your organization. However, they may not have the Visio application installed on their computers. It would be beneficial if both the teams share their work as it would save time and effort.

Object Linking and Embedding (OLE)

Object Linking and Embedding (OLE) allows you to place and edit objects in another Microsoft application, so that others can view the drawing without having Visio installed on their computer. Visio diagrams can be placed in Microsoft applications using the **Paste Special** dialog box. Linking a Visio drawing allows you to maintain the drawing in both applications simultaneously.

Linking vs. Embedding

Linking edits the object in the linked document without opening Visio directly, whereas embedding just places a copy of the drawing in the document, which later becomes independent of the original drawing. A Visio drawing might refer to a Microsoft Excel chart that is dynamically updated as data is entered. By linking the chart to your Visio drawing, you can include the chart as an integral part of your drawing and know that you are always looking at the latest version of the data.

How to Link a Visio Drawing to Other Applications

Procedure Reference: Place a Visio Drawing in a Word Document

To place a Visio drawing in a Word document:

1. Select the shapes or diagrams on the Visio drawing page, which you want to place in a Word document.
2. Copy the drawing.
   - Choose **Edit→Copy Drawing** to copy the entire drawing and verify that no shapes are selected on the drawing page.

 Make sure that no shapes are selected on the Visio drawing page when you want to choose **Edit→Copy Drawing.** If any shape is selected, the **Copy Drawing** command does not appear on the **Edit** menu.

   - Choose **Edit→Copy** to copy a selected shape.
3. Open the document in which you want the data to appear and place the insertion point in the location where you want to insert the drawing.

4. On the **Home** tab, in the **Clipboard** group, click the **Paste** drop-down arrow and select **Paste Special** to display the **Paste Special** dialog box.

 If you are using Microsoft Office Word 2003, you need to choose **Edit→Paste Special** to display the **Paste Special** dialog box.

5. In the **As** list box, select **Microsoft Visio Drawing Object** to place the Visio drawing in the Word document.

6. Select the desired paste option.

   ● Select **Paste** to paste a copy of the desired drawing.

   ● Select **Paste link** to paste a link to the copy of the desired drawing.

7. Click **OK** to link the desired file.

ACTIVITY 6-1

Linking a Visio Drawing to Other Applications

Data Files:

Calendar.vsd, Schedule.docx

Before You Begin:

From the C:\084902Data\Sharing Your Work folder, open the Calendar.vsd file.

Scenario:

You have planned the schedule for the current month for your team. It would be better if all the members in your team have a copy of it. You email a copy of the schedule to your team members so that they can keep track of the updates in your schedule.

What You Do	How You Do It
1. Select the calendar you want to place in the Microsoft Word document.	a. Choose **Edit→Copy Drawing** to copy the entire drawing.
	b. Minimize the Visio application window.

2. Place the calendar in the document as an OLE object.

   a. Using Windows Explorer, from the **C:\ 084902Data\Sharing Your Work** folder, open the Schedule.docx file.

   b. Click after the text in the document.

   c. On the **Home** tab, in the **Clipboard** group, click the **Paste** drop-down arrow and select **Paste Special** to display the **Paste Special** dialog box.

   d. In the **Paste Special** dialog box, in the **As** list box, verify that **Microsoft Visio Drawing Object** is selected and then select the **Paste link** option.

   e. Click **OK** to paste the link.

   f. Close the Visio application.

   g. In the **Microsoft Office Visio** message box, click **Yes.**

   h. Click anywhere inside the calendar in the Word document.

   i. Place the mouse pointer over the blue dot at the bottom-left corner of the calendar and drag the blue dotted lines forward to resize and fit the calendar in the document.

3. Edit the calendar using Visio.

   a. Double-click the calendar to activate Visio.

   b. If necessary, maximize the Visio application window.

   c. Click the text **Meeting with New Client 9:30 AM** twice to select it.

   d. On the **Formatting** toolbar, click the **Text Color** drop-down arrow and from the **Standard Colors** section, select **Red.**

   e. Click the shape located on the 25th day of the month.

   f. On the **Formatting** toolbar, click the **Fill Color** drop-down arrow and from the **Theme Colors** section, select **Blue Tint 35%.**

 To select **Blue Tint 35%,** from the **Fill Color** drop-down list, select the second color in the fourth column.

g. Save and close the drawing.

h. Right-click anywhere inside the calendar and choose **Update Link.**

i. Observe that the changes made in Visio are visible in the linked OLE calendar in Word.

j. Save and close the file.

k. Exit the Microsoft Word application and return to Visio.

l. Close Windows Explorer.

TOPIC B
Convert a Visio Drawing to a Web Page

You have linked a Visio drawing with other applications. Another way to share your Visio drawings is to post them on web. In this topic, you will convert a Visio drawing into a web page.

When working in a graphic design firm or other large cooperations, you may have to update the company website regularly to attract clients. Rather than rework on the website content, Visio enables you to easily save a drawing as a web page, therefore saving time and effort.

The Save as Web Page Dialog Box

The **Save as Web Page** dialog box is used to convert a Visio drawing into a web page. Once the drawing is saved as a web page, it cannot be altered. While saving, apart from the main HTML file, all other files are created and saved in the specified location. The **Save as Web Page** dialog box can be accessed by clicking **Publish** in the **Save As** dialog box.

 The **Publish** button is displayed in the **Save As** dialog box only when the **Save as type** is **Web Page.**

 Web pages can be saved using file formats such as JPEG, SVG, GIF, PNG, or VML. JPEG, GIF, and PNG are file formats compatible with the older browser versions. SVG and VML are scalable graphic formats, which allow you to resize the browser window so that the web page output resizes automatically. These file formats require a new browser version.

Options in the Save as Web Page Dialog Box

The **Save as Web Page** dialog box provides various options to save a file as a web page. On the **General** tab, you can set the number of pages to be published and the publishing options. On the **Advanced** tab, you can select the desired output formats and the display options for the web page.

How to Convert a Visio Drawing to a Web Page

Procedure Reference: Save a Drawing as a Web Page

To save a drawing as a web page:

1. Choose **File→Save as Web Page** to display the **Save As** dialog box.
2. In the **Save As** dialog box, in the **File name** text box, type the desired name for the web page.
3. If necessary, specify the name that would appear on the title bar of the browser.
   a. Click **Change Title** to display the **Set Page Title** dialog box.
   b. In the **Set Page Title** dialog box, in the **Page title** text box, type the desired name to appear on the title bar of the browser.
   c. Click **OK.**
4. Click **Publish** to display the **Save as Web Page** dialog box.
5. In the **Save as Web Page** dialog box, select the **Advanced** tab.
6. On the **Advanced** tab, from the **Output formats** drop-down list, select the desired format.
7. If necessary, set the other options.
8. Click **OK** to save the drawing as a web page.

Hyperlinks

You can also save the drawing, as one or more HTML pages, with hyperlinks and other features common to websites. When you save a drawing that consists of one page, Visio creates a single web page that contains the drawing and any hyperlinks within it.

ACTIVITY 6-2

Saving a Drawing as a Web Page

Data Files:

Organization Chart.vsd

Before You Begin:

From the C:\084902Data\Sharing Your Work folder, open the Organization Chart.vsd file.

Scenario:

Your organization has undergone a few changes in the reporting structure. You have created a drawing of the new hierarchy and have received the approval of the top management. It would be helpful to the employees if the new hierarchy is posted on the company's intranet site.

What You Do	How You Do It
1. Add a hyperlink to the company logo.	a. In the top-left corner of the drawing page, select the company logo.
	b. Choose **Insert→Hyperlinks.**
	c. In the **Hyperlinks** dialog box, in the **Address** text box, type *http:// www.ourglobalcompany.com*
	d. In the **Description** text box, type *The homepage of Our Global Company*
	e. Click **OK.**
2. Set the page title of the web page.	a. Choose **File→Save as Web Page** to display the **Save As** dialog box.
	b. In the **Save As** dialog box, in the **Page title** section, click **Change Title.**
	c. In the **Set Page Title** dialog box, in the **Page title** text box, type *Our Global Company*
	d. Click **OK.**

3. Save the organization chart as a web page.

a. In the **Save As** dialog box, click **Publish** to display the **Save as Web Page** dialog box.

b. In the **Save as Web Page** dialog box, select the **Advanced** tab.

c. On the **Advanced** tab, from the **Output formats** drop-down list, select **JPG (JPEG File Interchange Format).**

d. Click **OK** to save the organization chart as a web page.

e. Observe that the organization chart opens in the Internet Explorer browser.

f. In Internet Explorer, place the mouse pointer over the company logo and observe that it changes to a pointing hand, indicating that the image is a link to another web page.

g. In the left task pane, from the **Go to Page** drop-down list, select **Page-2** and click the **Go to selected page** button to navigate to the second page.

h. Close the web page.

i. Save and close the Visio file.

TOPIC C
Print a Visio Drawing

You have saved a Visio drawing as a web page. There might be times when you don't have access to your computer and Visio and you need to look at your drawings. In this topic, you will print a Visio drawing.

As a team leader for a project, you may have to review the work of your colleagues. However, you may not always have access to your system. Rather than delay the process, you can review the drawings on hard copy and suggest the necessary changes, thus saving time.

The Print Preview Window

The **Print Preview** window is a view mode that enables you to view a document as it would appear on paper when printed. You can view or modify the document in this view to suit your requirements. It can be accessed from the **File** menu.

How to Print a Visio Drawing

Procedure Reference: Print a Visio Drawing

To print a Visio drawing:

1. Display the document in preview mode.
   - Choose **File→Print Preview.**
   - On the **Standard** toolbar, click the **Print Preview** button.
   - Or, press **Ctrl+F2.**
2. On the **Print Preview** toolbar, click **Setup** to display the **Page Setup** dialog box.
3. In the **Page Setup** dialog box, select the desired orientation.
4. If necessary edit page breaks.
   a. Choose **View→Page Breaks** to view page breaks in your drawing.
   b. Choose **File→Page Setup** to display the **Page Setup** dialog box.
   c. In the **Print Setup** dialog box, click **Setup** to display the **Print Setup** dialog box.
   d. In the **Print Setup** dialog box, set the desired options to print the drawing and click **OK.**
5. Click **Apply** and then click **OK.**
6. On the **Print Preview** toolbar, click **Print** to display the **Print** dialog box.
7. In the **Print** dialog box, set the desired options to print the drawing and click **OK** to print the Visio drawing.

ACTIVITY 6-3

Printing a Visio Drawing

Data Files:

Calendar.vsd

Before You Begin:

From the C:\084902Data\Sharing Your Work folder, open the Calendar.vsd file.

Scenario:

You have planned to go on a month-long business trip. You are scheduled to attend some planned activities during the course of the trip. Carrying a printed format of the schedule will be useful to keep track of your itinerary.

What You Do	How You Do It
1. Preview the calendar.	a. Choose **File→Print Preview.**
	b. Observe that as you move the mouse pointer across the preview, a red outline appears indicating each printer page.
	c. On the **Print Preview** toolbar, click **Setup.**
	d. In the **Page Setup** dialog box, in the **Printer paper** section, select **Landscape** to align the printer paper and the drawing paper as seen in the preview.
	e. Click **OK.**
2. Print the calendar.	a. On the **Print Preview** toolbar, click **Print.**
	b. In the **Print** dialog box, click **OK** to print the calendar.
	c. Save and close the file.

Lesson 6 Follow-up

In this lesson, you shared your drawings. By sharing your work, you enabled several users to use the same drawing to save time and effort.

1. **On the job, how helpful is OLE?**

2. **Among the various options for sharing the drawings, which one do you think is the best and why?**

Follow-up

In this course, you created custom shapes, stencils and templates, and also collaborated Visio with other applications. Doing this has enabled you to efficiently create complex workflow diagrams and flowcharts. You can also share your work effectively with team members and vice versa.

1. **Of the numerous tools used, which do you think is the most beneficial in creating a drawing in Visio?**

2. **Of the numerous importing techniques available, which do you think you will use on the job?**

3. **What do you think is the purpose of creating custom elements using Visio? When will you use them?**

What's Next?

Microsoft® Office Visio® Professional 2007: Level 2 is the last course in this series.

Lesson Labs

Due to classroom setup constraints, some labs cannot be keyed in sequence immediately following their associated lesson. Your instructor will tell you whether your labs can be practiced immediately following the lesson or whether they require separate setup from the main lesson content.

Lesson 1 Lab 1

Designing a Shape

Activity Time: 10 minutes

Objective:

Design a custom shape.

Scenario:

Your organization has announced a design creation competition for this year's annual fest. You decide to create a logo in Visio to participate in the competition.

1. Open a blank drawing page and draw five squares.

2. Modify the angle of the five squares.

3. Align the squares one on top of the other.

4. Draw a circle.

5. Enhance the shape using the shape operation commands.

6. Format the shape with colors of your choice.

7. Save the drawing as *My Logo.vsd* and close it.

Lesson 2 Lab 1

Creating a Custom Stencil

Activity Time: 15 minutes

Objective:

Create a custom stencil.

Data Files:

Emblem.vsd, Org Chart.vsd

Before You Begin:

From the C:\084902Data\Designing A Custom Stencil folder, open the Emblem.vsd file.

Scenario:

Your client has asked you to create an emblem to be stamped on their new product. You go about designing the shape of the emblem.

---

1. Create the *Stars* stencil.

---

2. Copy the cross and star shapes as masters to the **Stars** stencil.

---

3. Name the masters and format the cross shape using the **Fill Color** drop-down list.

---

4. Insert a new page and combine the two masters with the cross inside the star.

---

5. Group the shapes together.

---

6. Open the Org Chart.vsd file and tile the windows.

---

7. From the **Document Stencil** of the Org Chart.vsd file, copy **Title** to **Stars.**

---

8. Drag **Title** and place it at the top vertex of the star.

---

9. Change **Title** to *Our Global Company.*

---

10. Save the drawing as *My Emblem.vsd* and close it.

Lesson 3 Lab 1

Creating a New Style and Template

Activity Time: 15 minutes

Objective:

Create a new style and template.

Data Files:

Custom Template.vsd

Before You Begin:

From the C:\084902Data\Designing Styles And Templates folder, open the Custom Template.vsd file.

Scenario:

Your team lead has suggested that all documents created in your team bear the company logo on the left and the team name on the top-right corner. So, you decide to add these components to your drawings, too. You also decide to set a standard formatting for all the shapes in your drawings.

1. Create a custom shape by formatting the text and line styles.

2. Add the desired stencils to your drawing.

3. Add the necessary shapes and text to the drawing.

4. Save the drawing as *My Custom Template.vst* and close it.

Lesson 4 Lab 1

Creating a Layout

Activity Time: 25 minutes

Objective:

Design a conference room.

Data Files:

Room Layout.vsd

Before You Begin:

From the C:\084902Data\Designing A Floor Plan folder, open the Room Layout.vsd file.

Scenario:

Your organization's headquarters has moved the conference location to your office. However, the conference room in your office is under renovation. You now need to convert the training room into a conference hall. You go about arranging the room with your team members.

1. Align a chair from the top-right corner of the drawing page using the **Size & Position** window to the following coordinates:
   - **X** and **Y** coordinates to *20 ft 6 in* and *-2 ft* respectively
   - **Width** and **Height** to *2 ft*
   - **Angle** to *180*

2. Move the second chair at the top-right corner of the drawing page and place it to the left of the first chair.

3. Place the desk to the left of the chairs.

4. Move the multi-chair boat shape to the center of the drawing page.

5. Place the flat file at the center of the multi-chair boat shape.

6. Place the corner table on the drawing page with the following coordinates:
   - **X** and **Y** coordinates to *2 ft 6 in* and *-14 ft*
   - Verify that the **Width** and **Height** is *3 ft* and **Angle** is *0*

7. Place the PC on top of the corner table.

8. Place the printer to the left of the corner table.

9. Lock the PC and the printer layers.

10. From the **Layer color** drop-down list, select **04** and color only the furniture.

11. Save the file as *My Room Layout.vsd* and close it.

Lesson 5 Lab 1

Creating a PivotDiagram Using External Data

Activity Time: 15 minutes

Objective:

Create a PivotDiagram using external data.

Data Files:

Sales.xlsx

Before You Begin:

Open a **PivotDiagram** template.

Scenario:

You have been promoted as the Lead for a new project. Your manager has given you details about your new team in an Excel workbook. You are to address the new team soon and have to give them details about each individual's role in the team. You decide to sketch the hierarchy as a PivotDiagram.

1. Import the Sales.xlsx file into the PivotDiagram.

2. Add the sub-nodes.

3. Add data graphics.

4. Refresh data regularly.

5. Save the file as *My Company Data.vsd* and close it.

Lesson 6 Lab 1

Sharing a Visio Drawing

Activity Time: 15 minutes

Objective:

Share a Visio drawing.

Data Files:

Home Plan.vsd, Home.docx

Before You Begin:

From the C:\084902Data\Sharing Your Work folder, open the Home Plan.vsd file.

Scenario:

As an interior designer, you have designed a room to the client's specifications. However, you need to get the approval of the architect and the engineers. You want to mail a copy of the drawing to the architect and the engineers and also want to post a hardcopy of the same. You plan to post it on the client's website requesting his feedback.

1. Copy the layout and place it in Home.docx as an OLE object.

2. In the linked Visio drawing, remove the image of the sofa that is on the bottom-middle of the drawing page.

3. Update the changes in the Word document and save as **My Home.docx** and return to Visio.

4. In Visio, using the **Save as Web Page** dialog box, convert the layout into a web page.

5. Preview the layout and change **Page Setup** to **Landscape.**

6. Print the layout.

Solutions

Glossary

closed shape
A shape that is surrounded by a continuous outline, such as a rectangle or circle.

Convert to Walls
A command that enables you to convert shapes to walls.

data graphic
An enhancement feature that enables you to define the appearance of the data in your drawing.

data legend
A shape that gives the details about the source file used in the PivotDiagram.

database
A collection of data that is logically related and organized so that a computer program can access the desired information quickly.

Document Stencil
A stencil that contains the masters of all shapes used in that particular drawing.

drawing scale
Describes the ratio by which the real object has been magnified or shrunk.

free form shape
A shape that is drawn freely using the mouse.

gantt chart
A graphical representation of statistical information in the form of bar graphs.

hyperlink
A link that acts as a connection across documents or between two sections of a single document.

layer
A named category of shapes that enable you to group related shapes on a drawing page.

OLE
Object Linking and Embedding. Allows you to use information from one application to another.

open shape
A shape that is created from a line or arc, but contains endpoints that are not connected.

PivotDiagram
A hierarchical representation of shapes.

ruler zero point
The location at which the X and Y coordinates intersect.

scaled drawing
Drawings that contain scaled shapes.

style
A tool that enables you to define the appearance of a particular shape.

timeline
A linear representation of specific time period and the tasks that occur during that time period.

top node

The first node that is displayed when you import a PivotDiagram.

Index

Looking for media files?

They are now conveniently located at www.elementk.com/courseware-file-downloads

Downloading is quick and easy:

1. Visit www.elementk.com/courseware-file-downloads
2. In the search field, type in either the part number or the title
3. Of the courseware titles displayed, choose your title by clicking on the name
4. Links to the data files are located in the middle of the screen
5. Follow the instructions on the screen based upon your web browser

Note that there may be other files available for download in addition to the course files.

Approximate download times:

The amount of time it takes to download your data files will vary according to the file's size and your Internet connection speed. A broadband connection is highly recommended. The average time to download a 10 mb file on a broadband connection is less than 1 minute.

084902 S3 rev 1.1
ISBN-13 978-1-4246-0693-1
ISBN-10 1-4246-0693-4